Clan of the Goddess

Celtic Wisdom and Ritual for Women

By

C. C. Brondwin

NEW PAGE BOOKS
A division of The Career Press, Inc.
Franklin Lakes, NJ

CLAN OF THE GODDESS

Edited and typeset by Nicole DeFelice
Cover design and illustrations by Christine Ahmad
Printed in the U.S.A. by Book-mart Press

To order this title, please call toll-free 1-800-CAREER-1 (NJ and Canada: 201-848-0310) to order using VISA or Master Card, or for further information on books from Career Press.

The Career Press, Inc., 3 Tice Road, PO Box 687,
Franklin Lakes, NJ 07417
www.careerpress.com
www.newpagebooks.com

Library of Congress Cataloging-in-Publication Data

Brondwin, C. C., 1945-
    Clan of the Goddess : Celtic wisdom and ritual for women / by C.C. Brondwin.
        p. cm.
    Includes index.
    ISBN 1-56414-604-9 (pbk.)

    BF1623.G63 B76 2002
    299'.16—dc21

                                                              2001057928

Dedicated to my beloved
William D. Johnson

In Memory of Clan Mothers
Martha Elizabeth Wrigglesworth Snowdon Swinhoe,
my mother
Nanny Kitty Brew, my grandmother
L. Ruth Cassady Johnson, my third mother

In Commemoration of Clan Daughters
Linda, Shelly, and Melissa
Kelly and Katie
Christine
Tanya and Tasha

"It has been the belief of every age
that women are more frequently blessed with
the gifts of inspiration and that
the mists of the future hang less darkly
before their eyes
than before those of men."

— W. Winwood Reade

ontents

Introduction

The Clan of the Goddess

The Clan Mothers have exciting news. You, my friend, are counted as a treasured member of that elemental sisterhood of all time—the Clan of the Goddess. Indeed, you hold in your heart a lifetime membership-in-good-standing in this ancient clan, this all-enduring, longest lasting sorority in human history. And the Clan Mothers, those admirable wisewomen who teach and guide us, know you as a strong, courageous, and truly gifted woman—the magically-talented being that you are in your heart and soul.

Deep down, you may have suspected this. You have felt drawn to the Goddess from time to time, or at least been curious about Her. Perhaps you've been seeking the kind of female support offered by that ancient tradition of real sisterhood found only in the spiritual realm of the Goddess. And now you realize how much your battered and broken heart longs for solace, and for the reassurance you'll find from being close to Her.

Rest assured, the Goddess opens Her arms to you. Her wisewomen, the revered and respected Clan Mothers of the ancient world, welcome you back into the fold, back into the familiar ambiance of spiritual sisterhood, of loving and sharing. You see, the news truly is exciting—you are a valued daughter of the Clan of the Goddess. Congratulations, you wondrous woman.

"But hold it," you say, "who are these Clan Mothers?" Well, they are your wise female mentors. I knew them as my accomplished grandmother, the mystic from the sacred Isle of Man; as my dear mother, the diviner, from the old Celtic Welsh; and as my tiny Irish mother-in-law, the wise one with the mirthful heart. Their wisdom travels from generation to generation in the time-honored Celtic tradition. The Goddess teachings are passed down from the Clan Mothers to the younger women by word and by example, and that is the basis of my spiritual education and training.

Although it is the Celts who still cling tenaciously to the wisdom of Goddess teachings, respected tribal Clan Mothers weren't their exclusive dominion. Amazingly, anthropologists, archeologists, and sociologists have discovered that councils of elderly women, or revered wisewomen, were the natural and intrinsic leaders of prehistoric tribes in all corners of the world. Clan Mothers belong to all of us.

Worship of the Goddess, the Great Mother, was an abiding faith worldwide for more than 20,000 years. Imagine! And although many of these scattered tribes were not in contact, they all shared a common faith in a feminine divine. They also shared a primary belief in the interconnectedness of all life on Earth that the Celts called the Web of Life. This included a respect for the natural rhythms of life—the ebb and flow of the tides, the phases of the moon, and the changing of the seasons—and an acceptance of the inevitable cycles of birth, death, and regeneration. Consequently, they were well aware of the capabilities and the far-reaching talents of women, which did not preclude their ability to lead and to rule the tribe.

Followers believed in the existence of life after death and the notion that the earthplane is only part of our long and incredible journey.

What does this have to do with you today? Plenty. Belief in the Goddess is the basis of the current resurgence of a women's spirituality movement—that hush-hush, private revolution that is exploding, with great fireworks, within each of our hearts and souls. It is a movement of ideas and beliefs in a feminine divine that defies convention. It's a personal spiritual journey that steadfastly shuns the establishment of an institutional structure, restrictions, or rules. You stand proudly at the helm of your own quiet revolution as you forge new paradigms based on ancient truths.

By keeping the Goddess on a personal level, the marketing executives, the bean counters, the frantic demographers, pollsters, and other chroniclers of our times have no idea how deep and wide-spread this women's spiritual revolution—this underground Clan of the Goddess—really is. Let's keep it that way. The definition of your Goddess is your own delicious secret.

Membership in this quiet revolution first requires your recognition of the Goddess within you, and your acknowledgment that She is part of who you really are. Discovering and embracing your notion of the Goddess will unleash enormous spiritual power—that unique woman's power you have inherited as a true and beloved daughter of the Clan of the Goddess. You *know* it will. At times, I'm sure, you have felt yourself wanting to turn your face to Her, to the wisdom of a Great and Divine Mother. And when you finally let Her into your private thoughts, your secret longings, you'll experience a welcoming flood of warmth and reassurance. But knowing this isn't enough. How do you reconnect with the basic truth of your Goddess?

Help is right here in your hands. I'll assist as you gather the various bits and pieces of your scattered spiritual strength, and dust off the undervalued woman's energy that is the sum total of your personal magick. With the help of the ancient Clan Mothers, I'll share with you their time-honored knowledge, their celebration of all that's magical in life, and their Celtic zest for living.

But wait a minute . . . tell me more about the ancient Clan Mothers, those earthly emissaries from the Goddess. How can I know these amazing crones today?

The Clan Mothers of ancient Celtic tradition were an anointed circle of experienced and caring women, ancient treasures who have been sorrowfully lost to our modern society. They were the women who demonstrated wit and wisdom, and were dedicated to teaching and guiding young women in their careers, in their love lives, and on their personal spiritual voyage. They were kind, but firm, mentors. They readily offered a shoulder to cry on, a pat on the back when you did well, and the much-needed encouragement and approval that helped build a strong self-image. Where are they now, when we so sorely need them?

In part, they are here—right in your hands. You were drawn to this book because you want more information, more guidance, more direction on your solitary journey of spiritual discovery. I'm C.C. Brondwin, and I am a spokeswoman for the Clan Mothers. They speak through me to you, whispering their words of wisdom, their secrets, their herbal magick. But mostly, they speak of their everlasting love for you. They wish for nothing more than to see you stand straight and tall and full of fine confidence. They want you to believe that if you wanted to, you could take on the world because, in fact, you can.

The Clan Mothers will be cheering from the sidelines as you turn your attitudes upside down, and begin to understand that your survival of life's sorrows and pain is a woman's triumph—a personal victory. Not a failure. They want you to learn to use your unique magick to heal yourself, to enrich your life, and to protect those you love. But most of all, they want you to believe in the divinity of your own soul; to recognize that you are the Goddess incarnate, and that She is you. Wow. What a wild ride ahead for you, dear friend. Real empowerment awaits if you simply listen to your mentors—your very own fan club of formidable Clan Mothers.

You've always suspected She was there, haven't you? It's such a shame no one was there to reassure you of Her existence. No one was there to nail up the wooden sign posts of life, to turn you around and point you in the right direction when your steps faltered, or to pick you up when you stumbled and fell.

In your heart, you have longed to consolidate and expand all that power you feel hidden deep inside. You have a woman's intuition, of course, because intuition has often shown you the way even though your head said something different, hasn't it? And I'll bet you know there is more to coincidence, to *déjà vu*, and to that old "gut feeling" than most people ever allow themselves to imagine. You've known something was going on inside you since you were a little girl, haven't you?

It will come as a surprise, but you may have called on the Goddess when you were a child. If you ever recited the nursery rhyme, *Ride a Cock Horse*, you were repeating an ancient spiritual chant that was intended to draw the Goddess to you—it was your very first magick trick!

"Impossible," you scoff, "it's just a kid's nursery rhyme." Ah, but there's more to life than meets the eye. Come on, you can recall the rest of it. Nothing is ever really lost or forgotten. I'll bet it all comes back to you. Here we go, belt it out:

> Ride a cock-horse to Banbury Cross
> To see a fine lady upon a white horse,
> With rings on her fingers and bells on her toes,
> She shall have music wherever she goes.

Who was this mysterious "Fine Lady" you were so eager to join, to ride along beside on your own little hobby horse, as you imagined the tinkling of tiny silver bells and Her ringing laughter? Well, She was none other than the ancient Celtic Goddess, Herself. You were chanting, in the grand old oral tradition, about the universal appeal of the female divine and the natural desire you felt, even as a child, to be in Her delightful company.

From the description in the rhyme, you were paying tribute to Epona, the Horse Goddess. She was one of the most popular goddess images—a veritable rock star of early Celtic legends. Epona was even adopted by the Roman soldiers who occupied Britain during Caesar's time. They were so enamored of Her, they took Her Goddess image back home to Italy to worship. Now, that's charisma!

I'll bet you have a picture of Epona in your mind—a beauty with long, silky hair brushing Her thighs as She rides bareback on a gorgeous white mare. (Yes, She's the source of the Lady Godiva legend.) She was feisty and proud, and wow! Was She a fine horsewoman. By today's standards you'd have to say that the Goddess as Epona was "a force to be reckoned with." And by the reference to music, She must have been a fun-loving party goddess, too, for the Celts always loved a good time. They still do—and so should you.

"Aha!" you say, "that means the 'cock-horse' has secret symbolism too." You bet it does. It represents the magick wand or branch that witches were rumored to use when they flew off to attend their midnight ceremonies. During the witch persecutions, women hid their Rowan or Hazelwood wands by wrapping straw bundles around them and propping the "broom" up in the corner; or they'd stick a carved horse's head on one end and let the children ride it about at play. Your childhood hobby horse began its journey as a magick wand in disguise.

Now, as an adult, you've come full circle back to the Goddess. You went out in the world and fought the good fight, but now you are searching out something else: something more. You seek to develop your spirituality—your own degree of woman's magick. The "fine lady upon a white horse" calls to you, the ancient chiming of her tiny bells drawing you ever closer, to rediscover the forgotten mysteries of the feminine divine. On your journey, I'll help you discover the personal power that is your magick wand; and I'll introduce you to the best friend you will ever have—your spirit guide. I'll encourage you to set free your sensual nature, and to use your personal magick as an essential tool for living a fuller, richer life.

They say there are a thousand names for the Goddess, and I believe it. You may know Her Celtic face as Epona, Brigit, Briganntia, or Bride; you may call Her the Great Mother, the Higher Self or Mother Nature. She took numerous forms and was revered in many ways. But it doesn't matter, for the most important single belief the Clan Mothers taught was that the incredible empowering force of the Goddess is found within you. It is this belief that lingers still. It's imprinted somewhere deep in your psychic memories, maybe even in the DNA of your cellular body. The Goddess is not some vague entity floating around up in the clouds. No. Plain and simple—*you*, my dear, are the Goddess. You are all powerful. You are utterly divine.

Not feeling quite that way today? Perhaps you see your soul as a neglected puppy, or a shriveled prune? And though lately you've been thinking about developing the spiritual side of your nature, you're not sure how to begin or where to start. Then you've bought the right book, for I will take you by the hand and lead you to that all-empowering force deep within you that's waiting to be tapped, waiting to perform for you, waiting to raise up your spirits.

Be clear on this: **finding the spirit of the Goddess inside your heart doesn't threaten any other religious beliefs you might hold, for believing in the Goddess is the same as having faith in yourself.**

Just be aware that unleashing such a positive force in your life is bound to change you, for it is powerful magick. Knowing Her will fill you with fresh confidence and put you back in control of your life. It will enhance, even enchant, your daily comings and goings. Releasing that pent-up feminine power will make you want to strut with newfound self-esteem, or throw your head back and laugh one of those deeply satisfying belly laughs. You'll learn to shed the burden of guilt you've carried through life, the burden that causes your spirit to walk about doubled-up under its ominous weight. And She'll encourage you to enjoy your time on Earth: to eat and drink and make merry and—wink, wink/nudge, nudge—to enrich your sex life with more passion, for to make love was to honor Her. You'll learn a spell to renew your current love or, if you're in search of a new lover, you'll learn how to cast your net to pull in an exciting new playmate to warm your bed . . . maybe even two. Remember, no guilt.

I'll be your guide on Abred—the earthplane. Consider me your cosmic sister, a hereditary daughter and granddaughter of Celtic wisewomen, women of spiritual substance (now often referred to as witches), who raised me to talk to the spirits. They taught me divination, spells, and ritual—simple, everyday magick. Thankfully, I never had to eat stews of dried gopher tails, bat's blood, and eyes of newt, but I did come to know the power of talismans and helpful spells; the importance of surrounding myself with animal friends; and the comfort and reassurance that comes when you walk and talk with your own spirit guide. Even as a university executive and a national journalist, I never forgot to use the magick my Clan Mothers taught me.

I'd have to describe my grandmother and mother as thoroughly modern witches with one foot in ancient times and the other firmly planted in our world. Every winter, as a child, I wore a clove of garlic with the herb Angelica in a red cloth bag around my neck, to ward off colds and flu and maybe the evil eye. Every coat I put on had a dried rabbit's foot already tucked in the pocket, since the hare was sacred to the Goddess. I can still feel the cool, satin-like fur as I stroked it for protection while walking to school. During the two summers when polio struck our city, I was never without a half-dozen cloth amulets swinging around my neck to protect me from that terrible disease.

Magick was everywhere; it was part of my life. Even my nickname, "Lolly," meant "a favorite of the Goddess." To me, the line between the spirits and humans was thin. The women in my family taught me the awesome power of using my magick every day, and they gave me the gift of extra confidence that comes from knowing our women's secrets, our mysteries. Equally important, they showed me how to find the funny side of everything that befell me. I grew up knowing I was naturally "part witch" and you'll soon discover that you are, too.

You have that same potential to unleash the Goddess magick in your heart and you know it, don't you? You sense it deep inside. I'll teach you the Clan Mothers' brand of natural wisdom and ritual, their straight-shooting values, and view of the world. I think of it as sweet, everyday kitchen magick, the kind you can conjure up anywhere, even while bumping along on the bus to work. You'll cast spells for yourself and your friends, for all those you love and hold dear—even for your enemies. Yes, even them, for in strange and hidden ways they help you to learn and to grow. And you'll discover that your magick isn't something scary. Your magick is full of light and compassion.

This comfortable, second-nature kind of magick is taught through my spiritual counseling firm, Soul Investment. Women of all ages, all walks of life, come to me to rediscover the amazing depth of their Goddess power: to increase their self-esteem, to protect their loved ones, to stand up for the sanctity of our planet and to better their own lives. I'll be delighted to guide you along the way to rediscovering your feminine divine, your woman's natural birthright. And like the good Celt that I am, I'll remind you to have a wee bit of fun, drink a flagon or two of spirits, kick up your heels, and have a hearty laugh at yourself along the way. Life on Abred is meant to be enjoyed.

My grandmother taught me that faith, like life, is ever-evolving. I could easily spin off a recipe for steamed hedgehog livers simmered in a rich broth of bat's tongues; or tell you to smear your menstrual blood inside an enemy's jogging shoes to get the annoying person out of your life—but those archaic methods don't quite cut it anymore, do they? We have to modernize: adapt the old Celtic ways without losing the heart of their faith, the crackling energy of their mysticism, or the playfulness of their culture. So, throughout the text, I've woven in work from well-respected wisdom-seekers of today, as well ·as some motivational techniques consistent with the spirit and intent of early Celtic beliefs. In this way, we will discover and celebrate the spirit force of the Goddess within us.

Once you come to feel the presence of the universal Goddess force within you, and begin to use the magick of your personal power every day, your spirit will blossom and you can reach out and attain anything—listen up now—*anything you truly desire!*

By the end of this book, the Goddess will have helped you find exactly what you need—whether or not you even knew what it was you were seeking. You'll laugh off the naysayers and be confident enough to do whatever you want: to express yourself forcefully; to stand up to injustice; to love whom you please; and to speak out for the protection of our planet. That "part witch" in you will open up and bloom like a fragrant apple blossom in early spring. You'll be fully recognized and enjoyed by everyone you meet as the wise and wonderful woman you truly are.

What are you waiting for? Jump on that magick stick.

Ride a cock-horse . . . ride, baby, ride.

Part 1:

Developing Your
Woman's Spiritual
Magick

integrity

honestly love

patience

kindness compassion

laughter

Gather up your special powers

Chapter One

Gathering Up the Magick of Your Personal Power

The Clan Mothers taught that when it comes time for you to die and pass through the mists to the sacred Isle of Avalon that we call heaven, the Great Mother will greet you. She'll take your hand and invite you to sit with Her under the dappled shade of the apple orchard. She will be sincerely interested in who you have become, and She will not be judgmental of your life decisions, for you have been your own judge and jury and no one could have been harder on you than yourself.

"Tell me your story," She'll say gently, "the story of your time on Abred, the plane of human cycles. Don't leave anything out, beautiful soul. Tell me about the wonder of you."

The unique and beautiful story of your life. The wonder of you. That's a clue. And the Great Mother doesn't mean tell me about your spouse, your children, your parents. She wants to know about your very own life. Have you ever stood back, way back, and looked at it? Woven from the richness of your heartfelt joys and numbing heartaches, sprinkled liberally with your victories and your crushing failures, molded by the love you were privileged to know and the losses you pain-fully suffered—your story is the very essence of who you are. That journey defines your personal power. It is your unique, one-of-a-kind woman's magick.

The early Celts believed that you have within you the power to shape all that happens to you. You have the ability to design your life; to create your circumstances; to influence the extent of your challenges. Early Druid sages and philosophers called it the right to choose, the right to practice free will. And you've been doing that all along. You alone decide who you will let into your heart and how fiercely, how deeply, or how compassionately you will love that person. If you listen care-fully to the wisdom inside, you will find all the tools to triumph over defeat, to heal yourself, and to create a life of happiness and harmony, if you so choose. What have you chosen so far? What is the landscape of your life story? What would you tell the Great Mother right now? What is the wonder of you?

Your life story defines you and makes you truly unique. Therein lies the strength of your personal power. It is there wait-ing to be gathered up, to be recognized by you for its importance, and to be used by you alone to help enhance your time here on Abred. It may surprise you to learn that you have already stood bridging the two worlds of Abred and the Otherworld beyond. "I have?" you feign astonishment. "I had a foot in the Otherworld? When did it happen and why didn't I know?"

Once you pause long enough to remember, you'll "know in your bones" that you were there and it will all begin to make sense. Here is the Goddess truth: humans are allowed temporary admittance to the wonders of the Otherworld when they experience bliss. In your lifetime, time and time again, you have experienced moments that were snatches of pure joy, of bliss. It was during those moments when your heart leapt, when you were full-to-the-brim with happiness, that you actually gained a measure of supernatural powers. With each experience, you added a little more divine energy to your soul and that is how you accumulated the divine energy that makes you so powerful today—whether you feel it or not. "How can that be?" you protest, "I'd remember traveling to the Otherworld, of being near the Goddess. It can't have happened to me."

Ah, you simply forget. I'll help you remember. Life with its layer-upon-layer of stresses, and the hurricane pace that gobbles up all the hours in your days, sometimes overwhelms you and blocks out your divine memories. In the maelstrom of reality we overlook our Otherworldly experiences, those instances when we briefly brushed the fingertips of the Goddess. Or, with administrative precision, we quickly and efficiently delegate those fleeting feelings of bliss to the back burners of our minds and they became nothing but a pleasant, though largely forgotten, memory. This is a human trait, and a mistake, but it happens to all of us. Just think of the daily stress you are under!

"When did it happen, where, and what is my magick?" Listen closely now, for here is your answer. Your personal power, your unique magick is simply this—it is the sum total of all the fragments of your life when you were blessed with feelings of pure joy. This is your natural mysticism and it is waiting for you to claim it. Your power is the accumulation of your happiest times, the hundreds of joyful experiences—brief as they may have seemed at the time—are the very source of true magick. Those moments were nothing short of gifts from beyond. To draw together all these memories is to identify your woman's magick. It's that simple.

When you go through this most pleasant exercise of assembling the bits and pieces of your own secret power, you will be stunned by the cumulative results. What's even better is that once you have claimed the whole kit 'n' caboodle of your power, your bliss, your knowing, it will never leave you again. Your personal power becomes your magick wand, your shield against dark forces, your conjured strength, your protection against injustice, your sacred healing tool, your friend, your helpmate. It will help define you to yourself by revealing the extent of your value, and it will surely give you the confidence that is your woman's birthright.

Your personal power is something no one else can see since it resides in your memories, your own mind and heart, and it is woven throughout all of your worldly experiences. It is intrinsic to you alone and it is ever-growing, ever-increasing. No one can take it away from you; no one can destroy your personal power. And it's all there, waiting to be gathered up in a golden heap on your kitchen table. Your personal power will give you the strength to do anything and to attain any goal you set.

Taking charge over your dark shadows

"What about all my bad experiences?" you are quick to ask. Humans are so negative. It can't be denied that the shadows in your life are an intrinsic part of you too, your flip side. And, yes, they ultimately add to your powers in a maturing way. But they are really designed to serve as challenges or lessons in your life, and the results of your dealings with bad or loathsome experiences form the foundation on which you stand, the platform from which you operate today. Because of the courage you showed when facing these sometimes death-threatening challenges, some of you may tower above others. But in all cases, your souls have grown from coming to terms with the bad experiences.

Step back out of your shoes again and, from a safe distance, think about all the hard lessons you've learned from your trials and how much you've gained. You'll have to agree that you are stronger, more mature, and more compassionate for overcoming the bad times. My mother used to remind me of an old Celtic saying: "the depth of your well of joy is dug by your sorrows." That means the more pain you've known, the greater your capacity to enjoy and appreciate happiness. Somehow, in your own way, you stood up to the hardships; you met the dark challenges nose-to-nose, and you were victorious, for you survived, didn't you? By harnessing the shadows in your life, you can disarm the most terrifying memories and neutralize their nagging control over your thoughts. In a later chapter, I'll help you develop methods to sort through the tangle of your bad memories and tame them once and for all. If you aren't already, you will ultimately become grateful for the lessons learned from the bad times. And after those dark times finally passed, I'll bet you greeted the return of happier times in your life's cycle with open arms!

To define the magick of your personal power, we must harvest the light and laughter in your life. It is the joys and small stolen moments of bliss that give you your resolute self-esteem, for they feed and enhance the flame of your soul and the enduring part of your spirit. During those times when you knew pure joy, you stepped through the veil between the worlds. You felt the warm, sweet breath of the Goddess. And now you will assemble those scattered memories to forge a steel-like tool of great spiritual significance, the most powerful tool you'll ever need—your personal power, your own magick. Now . . . let's get to work.

Preparations for finding your personal power

Your task starts at least a few days before you move on to your Initiation Ceremony—the ritual that will recognize and celebrate the consolidation of your personal magick. Assembling your personal power is sometimes a slow process as you forage through your memory for all the lost and forgotten pieces of your joyful adventures. But it is a beautiful journey of discovery. This is what you need to do in preparation for the ceremony:

Begin to recall the moments of bliss you've known and experienced in your lifetime: the moments, no matter how fleeting, when you were unexpectedly filled with sudden joy; when your heart leapt; when you got goosebumps; or when you were washed over with a warm wave of absolute well-being. This is your bliss.

Experiencing a memory block? Too many other things fighting for your attention? Take a quiet moment and hold a sprig of fresh Rosemary in your hand (you should find some in the vegetable section of your supermarket). Touch it, smell it, roll it between your fingers, and crush it to release its oils and heady fragrance. Rosemary enhances memory and clears the way to let your stream of happy memories through.

Most likely, you'll first start by remembering events. That's natural, and a good place to begin. Let me give you a personal example that may help clarify what exactly it is in that event you are seeking to zoom in on. It could have been the very instant you knew you were in love. Let's look at a birth event—that's falling in love. Even with all its chaos and pain, a birth often offers a woman that taste of sweet bliss. So, if you have given birth, recall the event. If not, focus on a friend or relative's birth experience or just follow along with me, you'll soon get the drift of how this works.

Remember the birth and all the details that you can muster, then seize upon the exact instant that crystallized a part of your permanent personal power. It may have happened somewhere during the birthing process, or perhaps at the moment of birth itself.

For me, my clear moment of bliss came several hours after the birth of my first child when the nurse brought him to my hospital room, handed me my little bundle, and left us alone. Cuddling him to my chest for the first time suddenly transported me. It felt strangely surreal. My head felt as though it were full of cotton, the room swam and at that particular moment, the world shifted ever so slightly. I felt it. It opened up a sun-filled crack in my consciousness and I stepped right through with my newborn. I felt pure joy and undeniable bliss, beyond anything I had ever experienced. Then it was gone. Yet that fleeting moment is burned forever into my soul. I recall it as vividly as if it happened yesterday, although the details of the birth itself are lost in a murky haze. That blissful experience is an important part of my personal power for I was allowed to see and feel a measure of my own mysticism for a fraction of a second, and it is mine alone. You see, even as I tell you about it, you can't possibly "know" my personal moment of bliss, or know how I felt crossing over to the other side. It is my own precious gift, and what a shame that I used to recall it so seldom. But not anymore, for it has become a major component in my magick storehouse now.

Let's look at your experience. It will be entirely different, but it is likely that the event caused you some new and remarkable feeling of being uplifted. You may never have spoken of, nor shared, your experience with others; maybe you've half-forgotten and simply recall the birth as a "beautiful experience" and yadda, yadda, yadda, who doesn't say that? So, here's the hard part—you have to go farther, you need to dig deeper.

The way you "go about" the remembering process is essential to the preparatory exercise. Here's how to do it: start by sitting quietly and remembering the sequence of the birth or other loving event until you strike upon that very moment when you felt bliss, that extraordinary flash of all-encompassing love. You're getting it! But remembering isn't quite enough. You may find that you are watching yourself in a detached way, like a movie.

The next step is to experience it again. To step right into your memory. You can do it and don't worry, you'll never use up that beautiful experience nor diminish it in any way. You own that magical and mystical feeling, but it is important to feel it again fully by stimulating your senses. Recall, through the fog of your distant memory, as many vivid details as you can muster: the textures, the sounds, the scents, the feelings. Think about how the light came into the room: did it slant through a window, or shine down from above? What were the sounds swirling around you: were people speaking, shouting in the background, or bustling about? Was there music? Or the impression of music? And what was the temperature or the feel of the air? Do you recall the weight of your newborn in the soft flannel hospital blanket, or the wispy texture and scent of your baby's hair? Were you hot or chilled? Was the baby crying? Mewing, or really belting it out? And remember if you can, more scents—baby powder, new pink skin, warm mother's milk—and were they blended with chemicals, or sharp and acrid institutional smells? In your mind, touch that new wrinkly skin again, feel the fluttering of tiny perfect fingers clutching at life. Go ahead, brush those tulip red lips with yours. Now take that mental picture, that scene with you as its star, and turn up the light so it is even brighter. Great. You are beginning to get it. You are beginning to remember.

And you knew in your heart that you and your child were transported somewhere above and beyond the mundane world, didn't you? Do you recall riding the crest of your emotions, of being lifted up? Did you feel, ever so slightly, the opening of your heart within your chest and the very lightness of your being? Live it again in your mind. Feel it. Enjoy the thrill again.

That joy marked the moment when you were in touch with your feminine divine. You felt the bliss of Avalon, the blessing of the Goddess. And even more importantly, you grew as a person. You became a much more powerful entity. Joy transported you to that place. Got it now?

Time to move on. I know you don't want to leave, but let's file those feelings away for a moment—don't forget them—you'll need them, along with many other powerful feelings and experiences, for your Initiation Ceremony.

It's time to recall other happy memories. See, the fun's just beginning. Dig around in that treasure chest of your mind for another joyful experience. If in your search you bump into bad memories or sorrow or pain, toss them back into the old trunk and say out loud, "No, not you!" Tell those memories they aren't wanted on the journey. Be firm and they'll obey you. They are your memories after all; you own them; they are your employees. Tell them they are important to you but the time is inappropriate, then forget them. They'll do what you say. They'll hush up. Trust me.

Go back and rummage around some more for another power memory—you'll be surprised how many and how varied they are. You'll find big important moments, far-reaching ones that changed the course of your life. And tiny, half-forgotten snapshots of your parents, your siblings, your children, or those silly laughing scenes that made you feel so good, so happy. And yes, lovers. Remember those fleeting romantic glimpses across a room, and incredible sexy encounters that lasted for long delicious hours. And haven't you had orgasms that lifted you right out of the bed and sent your spirit soaring? I hope so! These are all the ingredients of your personal power.

Don't think all your memories have to be as stupendous as the birth of a child. They can be of light and silly times, or be surprisingly brief in duration. Here's another example of mine. It was a blissful instant that caught me totally off guard, and I've added it to my arsenal of power.

Here's the scene: that same son, now a high school graduate. He's popular, bright and—you guessed it—he's lazy in school. His graduation finally arrives after much nagging, cajoling, threatening, and tense frustration. The run-up to his final exams was a tumultuous time, and I know you can probably relate to that on some level. I'm emotionally exhausted as I sit in the hot, crowded, and cavernous gym waiting forever for the graduation ceremony to start. Yes, he made it and he was accepted into his university of choice. But after the last few grueling months, we are all feeling rather flat, even about his good news.

It's been raining outside and the gym smells of damp wool and everyone is gawking around or squirming in their seat. Every footstep and screech of moving chairs is amplified by the high ceiling. My chair is one of those hard folding ones that's older than I am and too narrow for my hips. Someone directly in front is hacking and coughing without benefit of a hanky and that irritates me further. All I need is that cold! I'd really rather be anywhere else, and though I've been careful to pay lip service to my son's accomplishment, the lingering sense of turmoil colors and diminishes this final victory. Color? "Exactly what color?" you ask me. Good for you! It's a yucky washed out gray. I'm sweating under my spring coat and finally peel it off.

After several predictable speeches about the many wonders awaiting graduates and all that rehashed rhetoric from our own graduations, I watch his friends, one by one, troop seriously and nervously across the large stage to accept their rolled up certificates. Each friend accepts his or her tube with the blue ribbon, shakes hands with the principal, bobs up and down like a bird with a loose head, then scurries self-consciously the remaining ten paces before thundering down the short, wooden staircase. Will this ever end?

Finally, it's my son's turn and I crane my neck to see him better. He walks like the others, stiff and slightly embarrassed, across the squeaky stage toward the principal at the podium. Suddenly he spins around to face the audience, crimps his knees together, splays his feet and lifts his arms high to shoot us the victory sign with both hands waving back and forth, Nixon-style. In a great explosive roar everyone in the place cheers and applauds wildly. Spontaneous laughter everywhere. That little imp I so love!

And then, *zaam*! It hits me. That incredible, uplifting feeling of joy. His crazy gesture—this playful, joyful act—unexpectedly tears open the veil between heaven and earth. It raises me above life's petty concerns. My crankiness vanishes. A warm wash of well-being overcomes me. I still recall the feeling as if it just happened, and that's often a key. That comic moment is mine forever. It is part of my blessed magick—my gift from beyond.

Now, I want to blurt out a whole list of other blissful moments: the first time I knew I loved my sweetheart; the moment I spotted the white van barreling down the dirt road toward me, bringing my beloved daughter home after long, sad years apart; the indelible picture of my younger daughter at daycare, running toward me with both loving arms straight out; or later, as a young teen, standing before a crowd she had organized to commemorate Nelson Mandela's release from prison, speaking with such mature and admirable conviction that my heart was in my throat; and there was the crazy time I laughed so hard at my friend Dilly's antics, I wet my pants. I've got others. But the truth is you don't care now. You're off on your own satisfying trip of rediscovery.

I know that right this minute you are remembering something utterly joyful and fun, or maybe you are experiencing a tidal wave of jumbled memories coming fast and hard. Your job now is to explore each in great detail. Take it out and turn it over and over in your mind. Don't leave out a single detail. When you are certain you have relived that bliss, file it away. Oh, go ahead and simply drift awhile in the languishing jet stream of one particularly lovely memory, or race on and discover another you'd half-forgotten. It's your choice. But I must warn you, other magick moments will come tumbling out of your mind in great profusion, happy to be freed from obscurity and given the attention they so rightfully deserve. Gather them up like a great big bunch of colorful wildflowers to fashion your secret power bouquet. And don't worry about remembering everything at once. Power isn't static. More lovely memories will float to the top of your remembering, even after your Initiation of Personal Power. Rest assured, you may always add to your personal power to make it ever wider, ever deeper.

When you have a number of joyful memories, vividly recalled, you are ready to claim your personal Goddess power. In a moment, I will lay before you the details of a full ceremony which you can perform, if you so chose. Yet all these bells and whistles aren't necessary, you may simply cut to the chase and do a shortened version of the ceremony called, "Quick Minute Magick." I will give instructions for that jiffy method just before the ceremony begins. That's the beauty of your own journey into developing your natural mysticism— you are in control.

But if you wish to try the full ceremony, follow the directives closely: assemble your Tinder Box of Sacred Tools; follow the sequence of events; and invite in the bards and storytellers. Enjoy the preparations and give the Initiation Ceremony—this discovery of your all-abiding personal power—the noteworthy significance it deserves. Then the Initiation, in itself, will be a beautiful addition to your memory bank.

Origins of the Personal Power Initiation

There are a number of rituals and initiations into the mysteries that were used by ancient Druids and Celtic Clan Mothers. Most are shrouded in secrecy, and some components have been misunderstood or lost to time. Some women's circles today re-enact the parts they have researched, but the results are sometimes fragmented or sound awkward. The most effective gathering up of a woman's personal power, I have found, incorporates the spirit of the early Celtic ceremonies and borrows some methods from a contemporary exercise in empowerment that was actually taught to me by a friend, a woman named Eroca, with incredible powers of her own. Eroca is a natural healer and a constant explorer. She is known for always getting what she desires—for herself, and for all the many people she loves. She is part Celt and, like the Celts, she is devoted to intellectual and spiritual growth. Eroca accumulates knowledge the way some people gather pretty shells along the shore, it is part of her personality and it has added immensely to her far-reaching powers. Eroca is sometimes a teacher of mine and sometimes a student, as I am to her. It has been a very beneficial friendship for both of us, and we've grown from the experience of knowing one another.

Years ago, she was a student of motivational and behavioral processes, one of which is called Neuro-Linguistics Programming (NLP). She studied these methods ardently, adding them to her wisdom. One confidence-building exercise that Eroca mastered is called the Golden Circle. It was so close to the Clan Mothers' methods of empowerment that I've adapted part of that exercise to complement the authentic Celtic traditions which encourage women to find their own strengths, their own magick.

The entire ceremony can be done alone or with other friends of similar interest. I'll assume it is just you and me and the Great Mother. Thanks be, Eroca.

You're ready now; let's strike up the band.

Claim your own Magick

Chapter Two

Initiation Ceremony to Claim Your Magick

A prominent psychiatrist, Dr. Carl A. Hammerschlag, worked among Native Americans in the Southwest. He wrote about the importance of ritual in his book, *Dancing Healers*:

"Ritual allows us to attach ourselves to the sacred. Sacraments permit us to see and to feel the holy. Corn pollen, sweet grass, incense, rosaries, prayer shawls—they all help us to separate the sacred from the profane or the ordinary."

Our ceremony follows the flow of ancient Celtic initiations, without the secret tests and dangers that were a built-in part of their rituals. For instance, you'll be relieved to learn that you won't be expected to sip the mood-altering drink from the hollow of a human skull, as they did in initiations of yesteryear. I'll spare you that. Besides, wherever would you find such a macabre drinking vessel? The thought makes my skin crawl.

What is included in the following ceremony are all the time-tested trappings: the presence of the Celtic bard and the storyteller; the herbal potions and protections; the smoky incense; the Cauldron of Regeneration; the elements of Fire, Air, Water, and Earth; the ever-present flagon of spirits; the mood-altering drink called Witch's Brew; and the various sacred tools you'll need for a successful initiation. And be sure to bring your concentration, for a mystical experience involves all the senses.

Oh, one more thing—the mind is a wonderful creation. If you haven't the time to carry out the ceremony, live and in person, you can experience it fully in your imagination. Here are Quick Minute Magick instructions on what is absolutely necessary to include in the ritual, if you should choose to experience it solely in your mind. Enjoy your exploratory journey as you claim your magick.

Quick Minute Magick: Personal Power Initiation

For those who are in a hurry, or find it inconvenient to perform the full ceremony, follow this shortcut: With Quick Minute Magick, you'll reap the same fine results.

If you are sitting in a train, or on a plane, or stretched out at the beach reading this and want to gather up your personal power right now, you most certainly can. All you need do is read through the ceremony and imagine, with conviction, that you're doing it. Believe you are home in your living room and you will be—dancing barefoot, a lovely long gown of wine-colored velvet swirling over your sweetly perfumed nakedness (initiations are such fun). Concentration is the key. Remember, the powers of the imagination and intellect are far-reaching, well beyond the borders of what we see or understand.

But make special note of the Spell of Protection, read it carefully and do it. **It is imperative that you cast this spell about yourself even with the Quick Minute Magick.** Don't leave out the white light of protection and higher vibrations.

Later, during the ceremony itself, when you reach the part about the Power Fist—the action to lock in your magick power—say the words, "Mother-Mine," with enthusiasm and feel your nails bite in the flesh on your palm. Stay with me on this one, it will all make sense when you get there.

Other than those vital cautions, simply read along and imagine yourself in the center of the Initiation. Conjure up the setting, whisper the words that should be spoken, imagine the sound of haunting Celtic songs and the sharp, spicy fragrance of incense tweaking your nostrils. Feel the rock grow warm in your hand, and picture the ring of golden light before you. Clap your hands, noiselessly if you must, but clap for all you have achieved. Relax and enjoy your sacred ceremony, for it is yours to have and hold forevermore.

Components needed for your ceremony

Now for those willing and able to enact the ceremony step-by-step, it's time to gather up your Tinder Box of Sacred Tools specially designed to ensure success.

A Tinder Box was an ancient kit holding a little dry kindling, flint, and steel that was used to strike a new fire alive—anywhere, anytime. Care for the Tinder Box was designated as an honor because it held the means not only of survival, but of continued health and vitality. Your Tinder Box does the same, for it ignites the fires of your spirit. It contains all the things you'll need to prepare for a successful Initiation Ceremony. It's a tool kit, a recipe of sorts, and a supernatural road map—all rolled neatly into one.

Tinder Box of Sacred Tools
Personal Power Initiation

Costume: Anything comfortable that makes you feel elegant and powerful. Something long, loose, and flowing would be a good choice.

Cauldron: 1 cup fresh milk and a small handful of dried Sage and Basil to add to your purification bath.

Witch's Brew: Tea made from 2 Tbsp. each of fresh or dried Borage, Chamomile, or a small handful of fresh herbs if you are lucky enough to find them.

Incense: 1 stick of any spicy fragrance containing Pine. If made from scratch, include Horehound and Basil.

Candles: 6-12 white candles. Some may be tea candles in glass holders. 1 white candle beside the Cauldron (your bathtub).

Elements: Fire –the candles mentioned above. Earth –1 newly found rock of any description that you seek out to use in your ceremony, or a favorite rock from your own collection. Water –1 small pitcher of fresh water (tap or purified). Air –Your blessed breath.

Flagon: 1 bottle of Mead, or white wine (or white grape juice) with a small scoop of honey.

Storyteller: A *Riverdance* or *Lord of the Dance* video.

Celtic Bard: Loreena McKennitt's *Mask and the Mirror* or one of her other great recordings.

Discovery: If you don't already know, find out exactly where the directions North, East, South, and West are in your living room.

Setting up your ceremony

Chose a comfortable and private place. (For this book's purposes, we'll stage it in your living room.) Take the phone off the hook and tell others in the house not to disturb you.

Gather the ceremonial tools around a comfortable chair—making sure there is a clear space in front of the chair so you can stand without interference. The ceremonial tools include: the Element representations (unlit candles, rock, pitcher of water, and your sweet breath); the flagon of spirits; the music in the stereo, and the video in the player all ready to go.

In the kitchen, assemble the ingredients required to make your Witch's Brew tea.

In the bathroom, place the Cauldron ingredients (Sage, Basil & milk), the candle, and the incense on a low table or on the floor near the bathtub. Hang your ceremonial costume behind the door or drape it over a towel rack.

When to perform your ceremony

The Initiation Ceremony recognizes and consolidates your woman's magick once you have gathered together all your blissful power memories. You may carry out the ceremony at any time of the day or night. Celtic ceremonies were often held out in the open in a wooded (usually oak) grove under Mother Moon's smiling face, but magick can and does happen anywhere, anytime. Exercising your personal power is an everyday tool, so a cloak of darkness isn't necessary.

Someday, when you are well-acquainted and comfortable with your personal power, you may wish to carry out a ceremony on a warm summer's night under the enchanting presence of a full moon, just as the Daughters of the Clan of the Goddess did. But for now, choose an unhurried, convenient time that suits your timetable.

In advance of the ceremony

One hour before: Fix your protection in place

Cauldron: The Cauldron of Regeneration was a large sacred pot under which a fire, tended by nine dedicated priestesses, was kept burning at all times. The Clan Mothers used its mysterious liquids for healing, for secret ritual ceremonies, and for divining. Celtic legend tells that the waters of the Cauldron could restore slain warriors and cure the sick and wounded, while uplifting the soul and giving it renewed health and vigor. Quite an accomplishment for ancient aromatherapy! In early initiations, novitiates were submerged in its warm herbal waters. Your bathtub will serve as the Cauldron of Regeneration.

First, fill the tub with comfortably hot water and add a handful of crushed fresh Sage leaves and another of Sweet Basil. Sage is known to relieve dull or heavy spirits and Basil is an herb of novices. They both offer protection and counter any negative energies. Basil also frees you from any fears of psychic visions, so you can sit back, relax, and enjoy this journey without apprehension.

If it's the wrong time of year for fresh herbs, sprinkle a heaping tablespoon each of dried herbs from your spice rack. Pinch the fresh leaves, or rub the dried ones between your fingers, to release their power before scattering across the water, or use a few drops of their essential oils.

A word about using herbs in the bath—you can put the herbs in a net bag and swish it about in the warm water, use some or all as essential oils, or let the loose leaves swirl around your body. Simply scoop them out of the tub with your hand or a sieve later. (You might invest in one of those small wire mesh screens that fits in the tub drain, they're *de rigueur* for any busy cauldron.)

Now add a cup of milk. It doesn't have to be any specific kind, for all milk has powerful symbolism. Ever since ancient times, milk has been considered an effective protective substance and a purifier at the same time.

Ancient Celts, especially the Irish, held great store in Milk's soul-cleansing attributes and its wide-ranging abilities to heal. Women left a bowl out at night to keep the house faeries content. Celtic women used it to soften and beautify the skin, and Old Irish Myths claim it can even neutralize poisons. Powerful stuff this common milk!

Swirl the milk around counter-clockwise to release any unwanted influences. For a moment, dwell on the nurturing benefits of mother's milk. If you have ever nursed a baby, take this moment to recall the thrill of those cherub lips pulling on your swollen nipple and filling you both with love.

Set a candle to the side of the tub and burn some incense in a holder. As for the incense, any gently smoking fragrance (the spicier, the better) will do, but Pine will definitely clear the atmosphere and allow the positive forces to come shining through. If you want to get into the mystical trappings of ceremony seriously, consider making your own incense. I've included instructions in the appendix for making it in your kitchen, just as your great grandmothers did. If you do, include some Horehound and extra Basil in the mixture, for these herbs are said to give novices strength of vision and courage in ceremonies.

How committed to detail you get is up to you. The results don't suffer for lack of it, but if you feel ceremonial trappings will set the ritual above the ordinary, then go for it! Using the complete Tinder Box will enhance the pleasure of the ritual, just as a long, elegant gown will heighten the sensual experience and make it that much more meaningful and memorable for you.

When you climb into your milky bath, relax and let all your tension go. Lie back and recall your joyful experiences. If any dark memories try to muscle in, tell them to take a hike. Imagine a television screen suddenly shut off—*click*! Show's over. You have this power. Only love and light are invited to participate in your Personal Power Initiation.

Now is a fitting time to recall past lovers; not as you regard them today (banish from your thoughts any complications that preceded or followed the break-up) but as they were during the best of times for they, too, are part of your woman's power. Remember the intimate moments that gave you such joy—maybe it was the thrill of spotting your love outside a restaurant and how gorgeous they looked as they anxiously awaited your arrival. Your heart raced. Or get really intimate and recall the particular way they made love to you—their own personal flair—for no two lovers are ever the same.

Ah, the romantic and sexy feelings you had back then—surprise surprise—those secret feelings added to your personal power at that time. And it's not lost! No matter what has transpired between you two since, and no matter how many years have slipped by, echoes of the best of that love—the thrill of it—live on within you. Whisper a heartfelt, "Thanks be," to each lover for the precious, private moments of joy that were revealed to you. But don't forget to spend the lion's share of your time on your most precious sweetheart, and all the abundance and joy they brought, or continue to bring, to your life.

The Spell of Protection: absolutely essential

When you are relaxed in your fragrant steaming Cauldron, there is one more important step to do—you *must* cast the Spell of Protection around yourself. Some refer to this process as strengthening your protective shield with light. It raises the energy vibrations to help open your communications with the interior feminine divine, your Goddess. The Celts called this cosmic act of preparedness putting on your Lorica—your breast-plate of protection. A Lorica was like an ancient bulletproof vest. Casting the Spell of Protection is a simple but powerful exercise that should become part of your daily life from now on since it will serve you in countless ways. Here's how to do it:

Mark this page and please note: The Spell of Protection is essential before any ceremony and at any time you conjure up your personal power magick—at work, at a party or riding on the subway. Always bring forward the white light of protection first and wrap it quickly around your being. It only takes a fraction of a second to cast, and it always works. You can also use it to protect loved ones wherever they are; to surround a plane you are about to take off in; or to surround an issue, an event, or even a situation that needs help or protection. Simply picture what you want protected or infused with positive energy and cast the light around it.

protection spell

Close your eyes. Take a deep breath and hold it for the count of three, then exhale through your mouth. With each breath you inhale, see soft yellow light enter your body and begin to relax your head, then your torso, then your arms and legs. Breathe the yellow light in deeply and hold it for the count of three. Exhale all your spiritual debris, all your stress and anxiety. When you exhale, picture the air that is expelled from your lungs as black and sooty, diminishing on the next breath to a dull gray. By your third long exhale, see the air from your lungs as clear, unpolluted, and uncompromised. If you need to take more breaths until your exhaled air is sweet and clear, do so. Let yourself relax further.

Now imagine a cocoon of soft, white light surrounding your entire body, from below your toes to about 12 inches above your head. See it as a misty light made up of millions of sparkling particles. The light is comforting and it surrounds you entirely, holding you safe.

That's it, you are protected and your vibrations are increasing in relation to your level of relaxation. This white light will stay with you for the evening and protect you against any mischievous tricksters from Earth, or from other planes. Your impenetrable Lorica is in place. You are in control, totally safe, and marvelously calm.

Emerging from the ceremonial bath

Clan Mothers taught that the residue left in the waters of the magical ceremonial bath was contaminated with a lifetime's accumulation of the regrets and mistakes of the novice. While soaking in the Cauldron of Regeneration, the novice was released from the weight of the past. She emerged purified, renewed, and fully prepared for her initiation into the women's mysteries. That's you—magically transformed, rinsed clean, restored! Step out, pull the plug, and imagine all your regrets and all your mistakes whirling about in that tiny funnel, and gurgling down the drain. Bye bye sins of yesterday. Good riddance.

Now towel off vigorously. Slip into something comfortable, or a long, flowing gown if you are inclined toward medieval theatrics. But whatever you wear, forget underwear. Stay barefoot. Blow out the candle and carry the incense to your living room for the ceremony. Now go to the kitchen and prepare your Witch's Brew, that mood-altering drink of Borage and Chamomile.

About 30 minutes before the ceremony: Assembling the Kit and Gear

Witch's Brew—The Mood-Altering Drink: Borage is an ancient herb. Long used as a medicinal herb, it grows tall and lusty in the meadows and at roadsides, with hairy leaves and bright blue, star-shaped flowers that are edible. Borage lifts your spirits and ushers in all kinds of merry feelings. During the Elizabethan era it was said to "make the mind glad." It is high in Vitamin C and contains calcium, potassium, and essential fatty acids. It stimulates the adrenal gland and gives you a lift. It's subtle, but you'll feel it.

The ancient Clan Mothers had many a sure-fire way to chase away the blues. One of my favorites is the following:

> *Ancient Remedy:* For stubborn melancholia, take this remedy each and every morning upon rising, without fail: Pluck 2 or 3 live spiders from their webs and put between 2 slices of fresh bread, thickly spread with butter, and eat. Repeat each morning until the dullness of the mind lifts. *Yummy!*

Personally, after one dose, I'd pretend to be feeling so much better, I'd probably win an Academy Award!

Borage is much better. Gather fresh Borage if you are lucky enough to find it (be sure you have the right plant) or buy some dried Borage from your local health food store. If it is **fresh**, spin a handful in a juicer or a blender. From the juicer, drink about two tablespoons of the green juice mixed with water. If you used a blender, strain the juice and add enough water to make a half glassful. Make a separate cup of Chamomile tea to sip after this "Merry-Merry-Meet" Borage potion.

If you are using **dried** Borage, steep two tablespoons in a cup of boiling water along with dried Chamomile (or a good quality herbal tea bag) Let steep for five minutes. Strain and drink. Add honey if you wish. It doesn't take long to feel your spirits lift.

Immediately after drinking some of your Witch's Brew, turn on the video player.

Celtic Storyteller: To fit the occasion, dance will tell your story this day. Rent the *Riverdance* or *Lord of the Dance* video by the Celtic step-dance troupes that have drawn record audiences to their performances. The sound of their taps on the wooden stage reverberates in your chest; it mimics your heartbeat and quickens your pulse. Those leaving the theaters say they feel "high" from the experience. Watch it, or a portion of it, just before your ceremony.

Better still, be one of the dancers. Turn up the sound, get up and dance about. Hold you arms at your sides and let your feet go crazy. Laugh out loud and clap your hands with gusto when they do. Spin and turn and stomp your bare feet. You are wrapped in an ancient sound, long forgotten yet strangely familiar. How long has it been since you danced? One day is too long. Doesn't it feel good?

Dance as long as you wish. You'll know when you are tired and ready to proceed. Turn off the video machine and fire up the stereo. If the *Riverdance* music moves you, buy the audio version for your car. Surround yourself with the joyous feeling time and again.

Okay, Celtic step dancers aren't your cup of tea (I'm reminded of the critic who dubbed them the "storm troopers of dance" for their boundless enthusiasm and perceived lack of subtlety, I suppose). Well, you can rock it, roll it, funk it, rap it or pour on the salsa—whatever gets you up and dancing. Ballroom? Tango? Cha-cha? Strap on your feathers and do Swan Lake. It's your ceremony, after all. Just don't tell the Clan Mothers!

Celtic Bard: Loreena McKennitt's, *Mask in the Mirror* or any of her music.

For your Initiation Ceremony, I can think of none better than the haunting Celtic bardic songs of Loreena McKennitt, an internationally renowned singer, composer, and harpist of extraordinary talent. She'll lift you up and take you away from the harsh reality of today, back through time to the mysteries of ancient and gentler days. The first cut is a particularly good one for the ceremony. I wrote two historical novels about the Celts with Loreena's music as inspiration.

Flagon: Celts enjoyed their drink, and making merry was almost as important to them as breathing. Your successful initiation deserves an all-out celebration, so hunt down a bottle of Mead—it's honey wine. It was a favored drink of the Celtic wisewomen, for the bee was considered an emissary of the Goddess. If you can't find Mead, use a bottle of sweet white wine, or a dry white wine with a scoop of honey in the first glassful. Place the wine in a bucket of ice within easy reach of your chair—you'll be raising a glass after the ceremony when you kick up your heels in celebration. But remember, an excess of the flagon's magick turns it to 'demon-drink'—the downfall of many a brilliant and talented Celt, so savor your wine slowly and don't overdo it.

If alcohol isn't for you, chill white grape juice to near freezing, add honey and sip that. After the ceremony you'll feel naturally high. It's only the representation of the flagon that's important.

Nature's Elemental Spirits

> *Celtic priestesses always included the presence of Fire, Air, Water and Earth at all their ceremonies. As their faith was built on a respect and love of nature, the spirits of these elements were welcome and supportive participants at all sacred rituals, and were honored daily.*

In the same Celtic tradition, the four elements should be represented at all your rituals.

Fire: Set your white candles all around the room. They should be the only light so have enough to cast a cheerful glow. They needn't be new or slender or expensive. Just be sure they are all secure and won't tip over. Don't leave the room once the candles are lit and light them just as the ceremony begins.

Air: Air, that invisible substance that sustains us, is represented by the clear air in your body, a constant symbol of the Goddess dwelling within your soul. Reflect on the deep breaths that drew in the healing light and expelled the gray dullness, cleansing you.

Legend tells of the sacred Cauldron of Regeneration being kept constantly heated by the warm breath of nine diligent and devoted priestesses. The warm, sweet air circulating within your body fills you with that same elementary divinity.

Water: Waterways, rivers, and especially streams and wells, were sacred to the Goddess. Bodies of water represent the flowing fluids from Her celestial body. Natural streams and rivers were seen to be Her life-creating moon blood and the nurturing milk from her breasts. A representative of water is all important.

> *Sacred ceremonies and healings were often held near bodies of water or drinking wells dedicated to Her name. Fabulous pieces of gold and silver jewelry, with elaborate filigree work and highly colored enamel decorations, have been retrieved from the bottom of rivers and lakes, thrown there centuries ago as gifts of appeal or gratitude to the Goddess. These were the original wishing wells.*

Find your favorite water pitcher and fill it to the brim. Think for a moment. Do you know where your water supply comes from? Is it a lake or reservoir near you? If it is from your own well, give thanks for this gift from Her sacred body directly to you. If your tap water comes from a public reservoir, make plans to take a drive to see it, and to meditate on the source of the life-sustaining water you drink and how essential it is to keep it pure. If it is bottled spring water, think what a pity it is that pure water is not readily available to you. Now, take a big gulp right from the side of the pitcher, because that is sassy and fun. Drink Her in. Place the pitcher on the floor near you.

Earth: Bring the rock you specifically chose for this occasion, or pick out the all time favorite rock from your collection. I assume you have a rock collection, because the energy of ancient earth rocks is sometimes so strong they shout out to be picked up and taken home. If you've resisted their calls so far, start listening with your heart next time you take a stroll. Watch the ground for a rock or smooth stone that catches your eye, and respond if you feel it vie for your attention. It's for a reason—always a good reason. Take it home if that feels right, and rub that rock with affection from time to time. If it is small, keep it in your coat pocket, or add it to the vital earth energy of others in a saucer on your dresser or desk at work.

> *Stones held great magick for our Celtic ancestors, especially white stones or stones with holes hand-bored in them. Certain types of semi-precious stones were used for healing or warding off evil. Stones of black shining jet were carved into decorative beads to string for protective jewelry, and small sacred stones were sewn into the hems of children's clothes to keep them well, and safe from faeries intent on enchanting them. Every woman's home hearth had a number of stones tucked in the corners that held special significance to her or members of the family. Pet rocks were invented eons ago!*

Just before the ceremony, hold your rock for a few moments until it warms in your hand. Think about where it came from and why you chose it. Feel its energy and imagine it being added to the lovely energy within you this very moment. Imagine how many millions of years old it is, and consider how truly fleeting our problems are.

I used to wear a brooch to work during a particularly difficult time. It was a square of prehistoric limestone with a small fossilized minnow clearly imbedded in it. I would touch it on occasion to remind myself that all the pettiness around me, all the silly ego-struggles, were incredibly insignificant to the big picture. It worked. I always felt more centered and could rise above the turmoil. Place the rock, your emissary from Mother Earth, gently on the floor near your bare feet.

Incense: The lighting of incense for Celtic ceremonies goes back centuries and is practiced by many faiths. The smoke trailing lazily up to the heavens was believed to carry prayers, thoughts, and messages up to the spirit world beyond. The Celts used natural gums and resins to form dried herbs into incense cones, and had a specific fragrance or combination for each sacred occasion. When they needed the help of a certain "simple" or singularly powerful herb such as Angelica, which increased their ability to see into other realities—they simply crushed the leaves and dropped them on a hot coal, or slow-burning ember, and inhaled the perfumed smoke.

During your Initiation Ceremony, the spiral smoke of your incense, climbing up through the clear air, reminds you of the life-giving breath of the Great Mother and beckons the positive forces to attend you.

Let the Initiation Ceremony begin!

Note: You may wish to put another bookmark in this section. I will refer back to it as an introduction to many of the later rituals in the book.

The music is playing softly. Read the following instruction regarding the Element of **Fire**, light your candles and turn off the lamps.

As you light each candle, look into the flame and concentrate on its sacred significance to the Goddess Brigit. Celtic altars to the Goddess were often the family cooking and heating hearth. Since women spent a great deal of time there, and the Goddess was part of them, it was fitting She should reign at their hearth. Women greeted Her each morning when they stirred the embers and blew them back to life. Even today in Ireland, women draw a circle around the weak embers at dawn, asking for the blessing of Mary at the top of the circle, and Brigit at the bottom, before they blow the embers to flame. Fire lights both worlds.

Blow gently on each candle flame after you light it; watch it bend away from you, then dance back again. You have struck it alive and it bows to you in cosmic greeting. It is alive, yet a mere puff can extinguish it. The breath you detect by the flame's reaction represents the Element of **Air** for this ceremony. It comes from within your chest, near your heart. You are part air, part water, part divine. Don't forget that.

The candles are lit. You are seated in your comfortable chair, your heart filled with the stirring melodies of Loreena McKennitt, your Celtic Bard. Close by is a vessel of **Water**, your rock (**Earth**), the incense smoking away and the flagon awaiting the end of the ceremony. You are protected by the white light. You're ready. Now stand up. Rest comfortably and place your feet about 10 or 12 inches apart. Don't be nervous. You are the Mistress of Your Own Fate.

Whisper a brief and humble apology to the spirit helpers for any mistakes you may make in the ceremony. This is a universal gesture of respect common to many spiritual initiation ceremonies, including those of the North American Lakotas. Now, raise both hands high and say, "Great Mother, Forces of Light, help me gather my personal power and forgive any mistakes I make or any parts I leave out, for I am new to this, though my intentions are pure, and I come to you with a heart full of love."

Now, conjure up the forces of the four compass points of the Great Mother's earth. The Celts called them the sacred Airts and so will we. Turn your body to the North, bow slightly, and say, "North, I welcome the cooling breezes of clarity brushing my damp brow. North—the fisher's black winds and mystical Keeper of the Stones—join my quest, Northern friend. Welcome to me."

Then move your body to face the east and say with a bow, "East. Home of the radiant ultra-violet healer, and witness to the daily birthing of Father Sun. Add the power of your sunlight to my ceremony. Eastern friend and Keeper of the Sacred Spear, welcome."

Then pivot to the south and say with a bow, "South. White heat and white hot warmth, Keeper of the Shining Sword of Protection, home to lush tropical forests and birds of brilliant plumage. Come color me bright on my personal journey. Welcome, Southern friend."

To the west, say with a bow, "West. Home of the sacred Isle of Avalon, Keeper of the flame beneath the Sacred Cauldron, bring me the whispered blessing of the Goddess on your pale winds. Join me, friend from the West. Welcome."

Then say to all, with arms uplifted, "So as Mother Earth is One with me, let me be One with Her sacred lands, her winds, and her waters. Welcome all. Blessed be."

Drop you hands. Take a moment to breathe deeply and relax. Listen to the Celtic tune playing and hum along to the music, hum from your inner core. Make this request, speaking out loud, "Great Mother, fill me up. Let me feel Your beloved presence in the sweep of sacred energy we share."

Let yourself sway with the music and imagine you are pulling electric-like energy up through your feet from the dark rich earth beneath your building. Feel it. It is warm and tingling. It quickly moves up through your legs, filling your stomach and your chest. You might moan or groan as the energy fills you. That's fine. The ancients used to shout out with great volume to pull up the earth's energy. Do that if it strikes you. When you feel the energy reach the top of your head, move it in a circular motion and say, "Blessed be."

Open your eyes, if they are closed, and step forward one pace. Look down. Imagine a circle of golden light before you. It is about three feet in circumference and it hovers about eight inches off the floor. Close your eyes for a moment and see it. Wait until you have a good strong picture in your imagination. It is a shimmering, radiant band of golden light; a circle, hovering just before you. Open your eyes and step into the center of the circle. You feel surrounded by love and peace. Take a breath and relax, consciously relaxing your shoulders. Enjoy the healing comfort of the golden light.

As you stand in the golden circle, filled with the love of the feminine divine, recall your first joyful memory. See it, taste it, and briefly relive that feeling of bliss. Now give this memory a name—a simple tag name like "birth" or "first love" will do—any name. When you have it, hold your left hand straight down at your side and whisper the word that defines this particular memory. Then reach out, splay your fingers and pluck that memory out of the air—capture it in your hand. Make a tight fist, tucking your thumb inside, and squeeze hard. At the same instant shout out loud, "Mother-Mine!"

Done. That sweet memory is locked into your personal power grid for ever anon.

Now, recall the next memory and do the same, stacking one joyful experience on top of the other. As you say each name, squeeze that left fist, your Power Fist, until you feel your nails dig into your palm—not so that it hurts, but to register the physical sensation. Again shout, "Mother-Mine!" That is your trigger word, and the thumb inside your left fist is your anchor action.

Continue repeating the process. Concentrate, don't let your mind wander. Memory, following sweet memory, each one secured forever in its own Power Fist. Be quick! Don't linger too long with any one—just long enough to feel it, grab it, and squeeze it to you. But don't leave anything out, either, for each memory will build on the others. Every time you shout, "Mother-Mine!" from within your Golden Ring of Power, you will stand taller, your mind will be clearer, and your spirit will soar.

This is you. You've known and experienced all this beauty. This is the shining power within you, and you alone. You are the feminine divine. You have known the Goddess, time and time again throughout your life. She came to you and blessed you with joy. She held back the curtain for you to know the Otherworld, to step inside for a brief moment to augment your base of power. As the memories mount, your personal magick grows. Squeeze your left fist with real gusto. The sum total of these memories is the essence of you. You are luminous. It is the "wonder" of you.

When all your episodes of joy have been recalled and captured, take a deep breath and pause for a moment. Hold your closed fist out in front of you and say, "Thanks be to the Great Mother for showing me my power. I pledge to use it only for the forces of light and goodness. Blessed be."

Now take a deep breath and relax your fist. It is time to bid fare-thee-well to the Airts, the compass points. Turn your body to the north and simply say, "North," and bow; then to the east and so on. When you have come full circle after West, say to all of them, "Thanks be for your support, ancient Airts. Return to your home with my love, and my heartfelt appreciation for your assistance."

Step out of the Golden Circle and imagine it quickly disappears counter-clockwise.

You did it, dear friend of mine. You are fully initiated into your own special powers. You are blessed by the Goddess. Now you can leap for joy. Lift your arms over your head and clap your hands hard as though the curtain just went down on *Riverdance*. You loved it. All of it. You were the dancers, the audience, and the ancient music all in one. You are the sound of thundering applause, you are the Goddess incarnate. You are terrific.

Ha! You zany woman, you wild, unfettered woman—aren't you amazing? The Goddess Force smiles on you. The Clan Mothers praise you! And that unique magical power is yours to keep and to use. Your power initiation is complete, you are no longer a novice. You have come to know the depth and breadth of your own Abred power. No one can take it away. It will serve you well.

Throw you head back and laugh. Go ahead. Celebrate your newfound power, your gift. Raise your flagon in a toast to yourself. Feel great? You betcha. That's because you are great. You're divine. Start believing it.

Using your Personal Magick everyday

What happens now that your Initiation Ceremony is complete? Well, you have just discovered the beautiful secret. You can summon your power anytime you need it without another ceremony. It's fast and easy.

Whenever you want to draw on your power do the quick drill: cast your Spell of Protection; close your left fist tightly so the nails dig in; imagine the tingling feeling surging up your left arm and flooding your body; whisper, "Mother-Mine," with conviction and you are, once again, all powerful. Ready for anything. Ready to stand up for yourself and others. This is the base of your woman's magick. It will serve to protect you, and to help heal yourself and others; it will allow you to cast a spell of protection around anyone and anything, or to weave a magick charm. Your Power Fist will open the way to getting whatever it is in life you need and truly desire.

But like all new skills, it is *absolutely imperative* that you practice until it is both comfortable and automatic like typing, or playing the piano, or driving a car. Do the quick steps every morning for at least 10 days, plus anytime during the day when you feel the need to draw on the magick in order to cleanse and make positive all the cosmic energy surrounding you. Believe in yourself, in your woman's knowing, and so it shall be.

I slap your back in hearty congratulations. I wrap my cosmic sister arms around you and hug you with all my might. You are now an initiated and beloved Daughter of the Clan of the Goddess. You've just fine-tuned your powerhouse of exploding personal energy to work on your behalf, and for those you know and love. So watch out world, like our ancient rock star, Epona, you are a "force to be reckoned with." And best of all, your life's about to change—for the better.

Breathing Life into your Soul

Chapter Three

Breathing Life Into Your Soul

It isn't something you're asked every day but, tell me, how would you describe the state of your soul? What color is it? Is it solid? Luminous? Big as the outdoors, or small and wrinkly like the shell of a walnut? Do you tend it and nourish it?

If you're having trouble finding answers, chances are, your soul may be sorely neglected. Most likely it isn't a big part of your consciousness on a daily basis. It's even kind of funny to think about it in those terms, isn't it? But if soul expansion is your aim, and spiritual health is your ultimate goal, let's get to work on breathing some life and vitality into that poor neglected critter. Your long-range future depends on it.

We will examine issues of the soul and the Clan Mothers' teachings. You'll consider the health of your soul, how to shore it up and, most importantly, how to unburden it. Through the ritual called **The Goddess Unburdens You**, you will systematically release all the psychic weight and unwanted emotional baggage you've been hauling around all your life.

With an unburdened and unfettered soul, you'll feel light and spiritually healthy again.

So come along and learn to unfurl those fabulous feathery wings of yours. Recognize and celebrate the value of your soul, then be kind to it by freeing yourself. "Give over," as the Celts used to say. Let's not waste a minute more.

You want to know: How do I recognize my soul?

Here's one of those "Surprise, Surprise!" chants that I love to spring on you: "Ha! Ha! You just met your own soul." Yep. You spent the entire Initiation Ceremony operating from that very place, from your soul place. You did. The Initiation Ceremony, that exercise of gathering up all the blissful memories in your life, the times when you touched the divine within yourself, was true and beautiful "soul-work." Digging deep into your emotions and feelings isn't intellectual work, oh no, and it isn't body work, either. No way. You had a good old-fashioned, down-home visit with your soul. And congratulations, my sweet Goddess, you communed comfortably and effortlessly with your soul for what? One or two hours? Or if you did the Quick Minute Magick, just about as long as it took to read the chapter. And didn't that soul work make you clap your hands and spin about with childish abandon? You bet it did. The soul is a lovely place within. A joyful place.

So let's assign some time to get better acquainted with the soul. We'll look at what the Clan Mothers, the wisewomen, and the early Druids recommended for restoring its health. Then, we'll free that sweet soul of yours—peel off layer after layer of iron-heavy burdens from your narrow shoulders. Those barbells from hell that you've hauled everywhere—school, supermarket, workplace, doctor's office—you even lug them into bed night after night, year after year. How have you managed to function so well? You **are** quite amazing.

Soul sightings: Some can only see it once it's gone

Why is it so essential to give conscious attention to your soul? Because that is where the Goddess lives—your higher self, your immortality. It is the flame of your humanity and your uniqueness, and it will endure long after all the very mortal "dust-to-dust" rhetoric has settled over your cold bones. So, all in all, it's a pretty important place. And remember, your soul is now at your beck and call with only a squeeze of your power fist. That is amazing in itself. You never have to go searching for it, or be puzzled by it, because it's home—in your Personal Power Initiation you stepped right into the magick circle and claimed it loud and clear.

You are unusually fortunate to have experienced your soul so intimately and with so much clarity. Most people are never so lucky. Despite all they may have read about the soul, they are left wondering, bemused and confused by it. They are unable to fathom the workings of the soul until it takes its merry leave. That's right, when death occurs. Many people only begin to sense or understand the implications of the soul when a close friend or family member dies. Only then does it become clear, albeit in an abstract, shocking way, how important the soul was to defining everything rich and loving and lovable about that person. Joni Mitchell summed it up quite nicely in one of her songs, "Big Yellow Taxi," with the line: *"you don't know what you've got 'til it's gone."*

In other words, the absolute stillness of death tells us the soul has departed. The body is still there; we can see that with our eyes. And the brain that drives the intellect is still in there; we know that from our biology classes. But clearly, that undeniable spark of life is gone. And since the soul is the only part of us to continue its journey on another plane, it's extremely important to give it some attention. Now. Today. It is our only enduring aspect, yet the part of us we so often forget or ignore. The next line in Joni Mitchell's song was: *"they paved Paradise and put up a parking lot."* Not a bad description of the way some of us treat our souls, is it? We're surely crazy. And such bad long-range planners, too.

The Celts' strange customs of bidding the soul farewell

"Death is a strange thing, Sam. Dead is when the thinking and dreaming part of you no longer needs the body part of you. When the body part stops working, the thinking and dreaming part goes to Heaven."

—from *Sam's Story*, by Fiona Chin-Yee

Blessed be. Those are the words of a grandmother explaining death to a child in a children's book written by Fiona Chin-Yee called, *Sam's Story*. The grandmother in the story is all warmth and compassion. She reminds me of the all-knowing, take-charge image of the Crone—the universal wisewoman or Mother Goddess to all of us—and her explanation of death seems very Celtic, in that it reflects the Clan Mothers' understanding of the parting of body and soul at the time of death.

The ancient Celts, and to a lesser degree contemporary ones as well, have a strange reputation because of their odd view of death and their unlikely response to it. They believed that death marked the center of your life, not the end. Consequently they celebrated death. They partied at funerals and still do. This is mighty puzzling to most people, and even seems a touch macabre to our society's way of thinking and grieving.

It's not that the ancient Celts were happy to lose a friend or loved one—not at all. It was based on their spiritual view of us as multi-dimensional beings, and their keen awareness of that part of us called the soul. To them, the soul's spark was a person's essence, their personality and all the things that made them charming or honorable or compassionate in life. So, at the funeral, they celebrated the soul's ultimate release—its assured continuation—and the beginning of a new and happy adventure, despite the sadness related to the death of the body part of the equation here on Abred.

At their highly-emotional funerals, a Celtic bard would sing a specially composed requiem, extolling all the good works and courageous deeds of the dearly departed. Tears rained down, as the eerie keening of the women rose to the heavens, beseeching the Goddess to honor their grief and to comfort the mothers. The clanspeople in attendance truly believed that when the honors had been sung, the kindnesses measured, the triumphs counted, and the music had finished, the soul gained its freedom. Its journey to heaven began there and then. Charming idea, really. The soul lingered long enough to hear the eulogy and the final strains of the sweet music, then— homeward bound. Not much different from what Granny told little Sam, is it? This soul part, your spirit, is the numinous and eternal part of you. It is your essence.

The Celts traditionally spent three days and nights after the burial in a highly emotional and explosive state of grief, mixed liberally with celebration. They'd often fall to feasting, drinking, singing, and crying. Most likely a fistfight or two would break out, swiftly followed by hugging and making up. The entire event was a big, teary-eyed stew that has come to be known as the famous "Irish wake." From personal experience, I'd have to say that the wake provides a much needed catharsis for grief, finally bringing a measure of sweet peace to those left behind.

But you needn't wait to hear the footsteps of the Goddess as Death Crone, or the swish of the Grim Reaper's dreaded scythe, before you start to charge up your soul in preparation for the long trip ahead. No, indeed. You want to exercise what the wisewomen called the "Gift of the Long View" which meant being wise enough to enjoy life to the fullest, even as you prepared for the richness and fulfillment that awaits you after your time here on the earthplane is completed. In short, my dear, you should simply have it all.

Let me remind you of this beautiful fact: you are already miles ahead of most people because you have experienced the blissful power of you own soul. That is no small feat. Your initiation ceremony established communication with your soul and your divine Goddess within. You now appreciate the possibilities of your personal powers and your potential for spiritual development. That, my friend, is real magick. Now let's start to take good care of that priceless gift we call the soul.

Working some "soul time" into your busy schedule

It's time that you ask yourself: "Am I giving my 'thinking and dreaming part' the sincere attention it needs?" If psychic balance—of the body, mind, and soul—is what you seek, it might be time to ask yourself a few questions or consider some possibilities. You may wish to look at the activities in your daily schedule: Was there soul renewal time? Did you budget for it? Did you even consider it? Along with breakfast, lunch, and dinner, isn't it time to give your "thinking and dreaming" part some consistent and sustaining nourishment?

I know, I know. Your schedule is crammed full to bursting already. How can you find time for yourself, family, friends, good works, *and* your soul? Well, how can you not? Maybe it's time to reassess what you do automatically or, as we say, "without thinking."

For example: consider whether you should dash off for a pedicure at lunch hour, or spend that time reading to little ones in the children's ward of the hospital down the street? Which one is soul work? Or maybe ask yourself this: Should I do 40 minutes on the stair step machine; or, for a change, take a 40 minute walk in the country or in some green-leafy park on this gorgeous day? Feed the body, or feed the soul? "Hey! these are loaded questions," you say.

Don't get me wrong. I'm not saying that pleasures of the body are bad, not at all. They are great and meant to be enjoyed. Fitness and physical well-being were two important codes the Celts lived by—they took great pride in their appearance. To be physically strong and attractive were high on their list of self-pleasures on the earthplane. The tribal councils even had a special measuring belt with notches that was used to test the girth of people who were beginning to show a propensity toward chubbiness from too much sweet mead, or flagons of ale, or from dallying too long at the feasting table. If your middle measurement proved too broad for your age and height, the council assessed a fine and, worse yet, you were teased unmercifully. Yes, physical attractiveness was most appealing to the Celts since their codes of sexual conduct were, by our standards, loose and free. It made sense to stay attractive to the opposite sex.

The real question is this, and I think we both know the answer: is your time spent in a balanced way? Does your soul's care—its growth—count in your daily plans? Maybe you should think about it now, long before the "dust-to-dust" words are spoken over your inert body. Act now, while you can.

Clan Mothers rejoice! Soul health restored!

Okay, granted, you didn't know you were supposed to be taking care of your most precious gift from the Goddess—your soul. So you can't be blamed for not thinking about it more often. No guilt here. The Goddess renounces the woman's burden of "guilt" in any guise and any form. Regret and making amends are fine, but guilt is useless and a waste of time. Unfortunately, through no fault of your own, you've burdened down your soul over the years. Time and again, you have systematically heaped tons of emotional debris—doubts, fears, and guilt—on to your neglected soul.

Be honest, you feel a bit weighted down and heavy of spirit right now, don't you? Like most women, you're preoccupied with worry about someone, or with some on-going issue. Does that ring a bell? I'll wager it does. Maybe you're saddled with a sense of misplaced or undeserved family expectations that you can't, or don't want to meet. Maybe the job is getting you down and you're worried it shows in your work. Kids, spouse, meals, soccer practice, piano lessons, walk the dog, buy the groceries—busier than a one-armed juggler and deathly afraid it will all come apart one day? And your love life? Well, let's not go there just now. Pressures, obligations, promises made and not kept. Your nose to the grindstone; your feet flailing away on life's treadmill. Sound familiar?

Admit it, you've taken on a lot over the years. Life has been rough on you. So many unfair expectations in your past, in your present. So many to satisfy, other than yourself. So little time. But we have a way to make it better. To lighten that load and set you free to fly.

The Goddess Unburdens You is an old, time-tested cleansing ceremony. My mother made me do this very ritual after I had just finished high school and was working at my first real job and hating it. I couldn't stop weeping at the least little thing, and I was constantly tired. I slept for hours on end, even on my lunch hour. I began to feel as if I were outside my body, watching from on high, as I walked listlessly along the street. I was depressed and feeling down about everything.

My wise mother sat me down and said, "Your loathing for this job is separating you from your soul. You're walking about as if the weight of the world is pressing down upon your shoulders. You must go inside yourself to fix that." She told me it was time to let go of all the unnecessary baggage I was carrying around inside—the psychic weight that made me tired physically and caused this sense of separation, dislocation, and unhappiness. She lovingly guided me through the steps of the ceremony I call the **Goddess Unburdens You** and it worked. As a result of freeing my soul, I took decisive action—I quit my job and got a more fulfilling one. To this day, I still use the unburdening ritual when my "worry quotient" is rising and I feel the warning signals of heaviness and approaching gloom.

We women are especially prone to taking on the problems of others and that ups the pressure on us even further. Well, I say, "Boot!" to it all. I'm here to throw open the heavy shutters on your soul, to let the fresh air in, and set those sunbeams dancing a merry dance on the shiny oaken floor of your soul chamber. Open sesame. Let the Goddess breathe. Let Her magick flourish and enrich your life. What a lovely sensation. What empowering freedom.

In The Goddess Unburdens You ceremony, you will enter a light, relaxed state to help recognize the specific burdens you carry. You'll assign each person, each issue, and each hurtful memory the acknowledged value it deserves, for they all have some merit. Then, in the old Clan Mothers' authoritative, no-nonsense way, you'll send those old burdens packing. You'll banish all the worry and concern and unfair responsibility—the guilt—that has been bogging you down. The new you—free and light of spirit—will emerge with a fresh perspective so that you may totally enjoy the world you have created and plan to create.

Women's self-confidence: Celtic food for the soul

Confidence or self-esteem was an all-important touchstone of Goddess teachings for young women in Celtic tribes. Self-confidence flowed naturally from the high value placed on women's status in the community, but it was further reinforced by affirming chants, the committing to memory of empowering tales and poetry, and by the young women's daily education and training. These positive affirmations became deep-seeded truths, so self-esteem was natural and intrinsic to their very being.

Here is the sad truth about life today. We don't teach our daughters enough self-confidence. And our celebrity-driven society makes them feel less worthy and less attractive, essentially robbing them of basic self-esteem. This is the polar opposite to the Clan Mothers' positive reinforcement. It is sad to realize that even loving mothers today shy away from openly praising their daughters. Years ago, I had a woman scold me for telling one of my precious daughters how absolutely terrific I believed her to be, and what a good and selfless deed she had just done. This critical acquaintance told me it would "turn her head, and make her shallow and egotistical." Wow! What a downer. Can't you just imagine the Clan Mothers shaking their fists: women are to be raised up—not put down. But, come to think of it, how often were you praised as a girl or a young woman? Not enough, I'd wager. And how often do you hear other mothers praise their daughters? How often do you do it?

I always feel a swooping rush of the Goddess dancing joyfully past, whenever I hear women give other women open and sincere praise and positive reinforcement. This is especially true with "needy-souled" young women who are taking their first tentative steps out into the harsh and frightening world. We need more praise for women and women's work in our lives. You can contribute. Start today. Do you have a young woman in your office, delivering mail or in some other entry-level job? Smile and tell her if she's doing a good job. No one else will. Tap her on the shoulder and say "well done." It's a small gesture, but it will brighten her day and improve her self-esteem.

Or be a Clan Mother. If you have a daughter, a niece, or a little sister, go home and give her a bear hug. Tell her there is so much about her that is wonderful. Don't let her pull away. Hold her fast and whisper your heartfelt praise into her ear, then look straight into her eyes with sincerity and respect until she beams. You are doing the Clan Mothers' work. You are making a young woman a tad stronger. And don't stop there, look in the mirror and say, "Well done!"

Get on the side of encouraging confidence as a healthy act. Say, "Boot!" to the notion that it breeds vanity. Now, keeping the importance of women's self-confidence firmly in mind, take a further step and recite this most effective Self-Blessing Spell from the *Practice of Witchcraft,* by the late Robin Skelton, a witch, English professor, and accomplished poet. Don't turn shy on me, or consider this spell to be bragging or "over the top." It isn't. It's just the kind of re-enforcement the ancients gave their young women. This is a most valuable spell to memorize.

Here goes. Cast a quick Spell of Protection and put the white light around you. Don't forget to make your Power Fist and say, "Mother-Mine," to summon the Goddess and activate your personal magick. Then speak out the words with Goddess gusto!

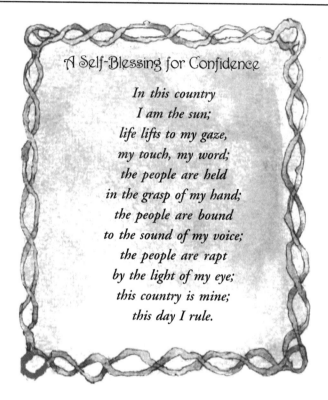

A Self-Blessing for Confidence

*In this country
I am the sun;
life lifts to my gaze,
my touch, my word;
the people are held
in the grasp of my hand;
the people are bound
to the sound of my voice;
the people are rapt
by the light of my eye;
this country is mine;
this day I rule.*

Wow! Are you powerful, or what? You rule! Don't be shy, this is important soul work. It's your soul and your life and you should be Queen of the World. Settle for nothing less. The Clan Mothers taught it and they knew their stuff when it came to empowering women. That's why there were so many women in positions of great importance in those ancient tribes. They believed in themselves and what they could accomplish. That's what you want for yourself.

Here's my experience with the Self-Blessing for Confidence Spell: I used to keep copies in my coat and in the pockets of my business suits, written on small pieces of paper. Every morning, as I walked the 10 minutes to the university where I was an executive, I made my Power Fist, repeated Mother-Mine to pull up Her energy, and said the spell over and over, shouting it out whenever a noisy transport truck whizzed by. Why? Like all of us, I was dealing with negativity in the workplace and all the accompanying squabbling and gossip. Unfortunately, it was slowly beginning to erode my self-esteem. It left my soul feeling washed out and weak. Did the morning recitation of this spell help? You bet it did—worked like a charm! By the time I entered the inevitable breakfast meetings I was a *Force!* I radiated so much self-assurance, I could relax and be warm and friendly to everyone. The Clan Mothers were right. With your confidence in tact, you can be your best in all situations, no matter how challenging. Robin's little spell is a sparkling energy drink for your soul. Commit it to memory. It'll set you up for any important encounter, and if you're just feeling low, it will surely banish the blues.

Now that your self-esteem is all fluffed up, let's lighten up your soul and free you of all that weight you've been dragging around for far too long.

Sequence of steps in the ritual

The sequence of events replicates those of the Initiation Ceremony with but a few exceptions. You may wish to refer back to, or memorize, the greetings and farewells to the Airts—the compass points of North, East, South, and West (or create some in your own words, since this will be a necessary part of every ritual you perform). Enacting this ritual will be easier and smoother, since you know the flow and rhythm, having already walked the Goddess path.

Quick Minute Magick: The Goddess Unburdens You

Be ever mindful of the imagined scents and sights and sounds and feelings. As you read along, imagine it's a full-blown DVD, surround-sound, sense-o-rama extravaganza. Let every step resonate in your mind: feel your body relax as you sink into the warm bath water; and let out a long sigh as you pick up a whiff of the sweet scent of Lavender and other herbs, bobbing gently on top of the steaming water. Feel the breathtaking surge of well-being when you finally, gladly, banish all the debris of your life's demands, and unburden your sweet, long-suffering soul. Lucky you.

As always (here I go again, nag, nag, nag), and this is true for **every** ceremony, ritual, or channeling you do with the Quick Minute Magick: be sure to make your Power Fist, say, "Mother-Mine," and cast the Spell of Protection to ensure that you are perfectly safe and sound, even in your altered state of the imagination. Enjoy, you Powerful Woman.

You've repeated the Self-Blessing Spell earlier and your cup of confidence is filled to the meniscus. It's time to pull your magick ingredients together.

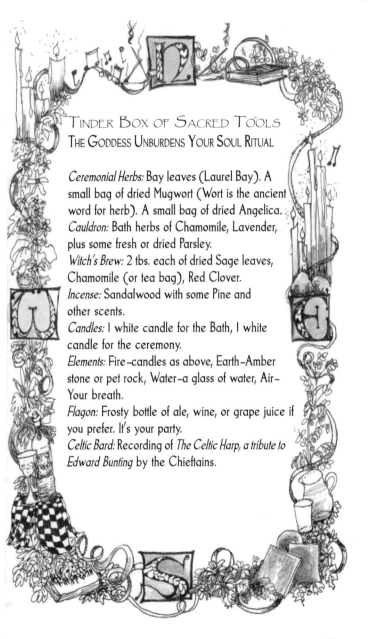

Tinder Box of Sacred Tools
The Goddess Unburdens Your Soul Ritual

Ceremonial Herbs: Bay leaves (Laurel Bay). A small bag of dried Mugwort (Wort is the ancient word for herb). A small bag of dried Angelica.
Cauldron: Bath herbs of Chamomile, Lavender, plus some fresh or dried Parsley.
Witch's Brew: 2 tbs. each of dried Sage leaves, Chamomile (or tea bag), Red Clover.
Incense: Sandalwood with some Pine and other scents.
Candles: 1 white candle for the Bath, 1 white candle for the ceremony.
Elements: Fire–candles as above, Earth–Amber stone or pet rock, Water–a glass of water, Air–Your breath.
Flagon: Frosty bottle of ale, wine, or grape juice if you prefer. It's your party.
Celtic Bard: Recording of *The Celtic Harp, a tribute to Edward Bunting* by the Chieftains.

Significance of the sacred tools

The Tinder Box of Sacred Tools contains ceremonial herbs chosen for their ability to calm and relax. The Bards for this soul revitalization exercise are the Chieftains, and their recording of *The Celtic Harp*, a hauntingly beautiful tribute to Edward Bunting. It's a collection of ancient string and pipe music, some dating back more than 300 years, that possesses its own stirring energy and magick.

The ritual purification bath preceding this unburdening ceremony is steeped in quieting herbs: Chamomile and Lavender, plus fresh Parsley sprigs (or a heaping spoonful of dried Parsley) in order to summon the maternal aspects of the Goddess. During this ritual, be loving and kind to yourself.

Set the candle and the incense beside your bathtub. Sandalwood is preferred since it calms you and opens the portals to the unconscious and the divine; it is a superior fragrance for all your serious soul work, and has the bonus of insuring success.

If possible, borrow or acquire your own stone of Amber. At one time, a diviner was easily identified by the possession of this fossilized golden resin. Its magical properties are legendary. To the Clan Mothers, Amber at rituals added strength to a spell, and helped deflect darkness in any counter-spell. During the time of the women's holocaust—the witch burnings—diviners hid their Amber stones safely away so they wouldn't be singled out. A friend of mine had a dearly-prized stone she says was passed down mother-to-daughter for untold generations, which she gifted to her own daughter on her wedding day.

Among its many attributes, Amber soothes the disposition and calms frazzled nerves. It warms to the touch like no other stone, has energizing and electrifying properties, and was once known to the Greeks as "Electron." Its warmth penetrates through the many cosmic planes to offer comfort to your soul and, in ceremonies such as this, it is added insurance to absorb any negative energies and send despair packing. Some people believed Amber to be the stone to use in order to keep witches at bay—how foolish they were! If we listen hard enough to the wind, we can probably hear the Clan Mothers hooting and giggling at that misconception even now.

The Witch's Brew tea is designed to calm and to bring clarity. It is made using a couple of tablespoons of dried Sage, Red Clover blossoms and Chamomile, steeped in boiling water for five minutes. Sage acts as a powerful purification herb, a virtual witch's broom to sweep away all the dust, dirt, and debris no longer welcome in your soul.

Red Clover was a sacred herb to the Clan Mothers, used in many of their rituals. It helps you get in touch with your inner self. The Celts loved Clover, considering it to be thrice-blessed: it served as a fodder for livestock; healed many human aliments; and its three leaves represented the living trinity of the Goddess and reminded them of her role as Mother Nature. The verified medicinal benefits of Red Clover are legendary. It belongs in your healing cupboard because it builds strength and physical vitality with its anti-inflammatory properties. Besides its impeccable reputation, it is naturally sweet-tasting. While strolling through meadows, I often shoo away the bees and pluck the red flowers right off the stalks to pop in my mouth. Ancient candy.

The Chamomile in your hot infusion comforts, soothes, and relieves pain of the body and the heart, while assuring success in your ritual. Drink one cup of this specially formulated Witch's Brew and feel warmth and relaxation spread through your body and mind. Life is pretty good.

As an aside: It's probably time to visit a good health food store that carries a broad range of dried herbs. I've included a shopping list in the back of the book so you'll be well equipped for all the personal power rituals in the following chapters. For the long term, you may consider planting a Healing Herbal Garden next spring, close to the kitchen or on the window sill. Still, dried herbs are fine. It is really the sincere intent you bring to the ceremonies that enlivens the energy and activates the ingredients in the herbs, and in you.

Preparation for The Goddess Unburdens You Ceremony

Time to set the stage. Place your representations of the elements around your chair (the glass of water, the Amber or stone, and the candle). Set the candle close by but not yet lit; put on the music and use it as soft background for your bath; put the ceremonial herbs (Mugwort and Angelica) mixed in a bowl close to your chair (but keep the Bay Leaves separate and to the side); set your ale, white wine, or juice in a bucket of ice.

In the kitchen, set out the makings for your Witch's Brew tea.

Hang up your costume and prepare your purification bath: fill the tub and add the bath herbs (Chamomile, Lavender and Parsley sprigs); set up and light the Sandalwood incense; light the candle and turn off the light; slip off your clothes and run your hands down your sides all the way to your feet in homage to your gift of a fine body; then step into the bath and sink into the luxury of the Cauldron of Regeneration. Whisper a heartfelt, "Thanks Be" to the Great Mother and all the Forces of Good.

The Spell of Protection

Normally, you would cast the Spell of Protection just before you start your ceremony. But not this time. Since you will be bringing to mind some unpleasant memories of personal burdens, undue responsibilities, and unfair expectations, you need it now. Cast it around your body in the bath and you can begin the process of sorting through those burdens with full confidence.

Now it is time to think about the ritual before you. Since you will be examining your burdens, you do not want to linger over these memories. Just visit them lightly, make a mental check beside each one, add it to your disposal list, and move on. You don't want to give these burdens any additional energy. It is especially important not to amplify the sadness that may surround some of them. It is enough that you see and recognize them for what they are.

What kind of burdens do you need to release?

You'll recognize many of your lifetime burdens in a flash—*Wow! I've been carrying this incredible psychic weight for a long, long time.* Time to show it the door!

Yet some burdens may not be so readily apparent. Why? Because they masquerade as a way for other people to define you, or even worse, to restrict you. Being a "doormat" to boyfriends might be an example. You may have come to accept this negative definition of yourself, rather than see it as a burden you took on somewhere along the line by giving away too much in a bad relationship. If that is the case, get rid of it. Don't embrace and accept such a burden. Don't live it any longer.

Other burdens you carry may come just by the luck of the draw. For example, the birth position in your family is loaded with built-in burdens. Were you an only child, pampered and indulged on the one hand, but also saddled with all the family's expectations, obligations, and responsibilities? Maybe a hefty dose of loneliness and isolation were part of the mix, too. If so, do you still carry that weight and does it permeate your life and affect it adversely? Would you like to be finally free of that burden. Yes? Then name it and put it in the lineup for ritual cleansing.

Were you a middle child always vying for attention? Perhaps you were born the youngest or considered the "favorite" and had to endure the wrath of your older siblings. Or maybe, despite where you stood in the line, you somehow felt an obligation to make up to your parents for another sibling's failings or transgressions; or you felt compelled to entertain and amuse. You get the idea? You need to start here, in your childhood.

But issues and slights and unfair role responsibilities aren't the only baggage you lug about. You may feel unduly responsible for the welfare of certain family members. If you are a new immigrant or the child of immigrants, your burden may include an entire nation or culture left behind, perhaps one that has been unjustly persecuted. That's a lot of tonnage for your narrow human shoulders, isn't it? Too much, really. Chances are you assumed this burden as a child; it's time to unload much of it.

There will be starting discoveries. In my unburdening ceremony, I was surprised to find that I still carried the weight of a loved one I had felt responsible for decades before. Though this relative no longer needed me—he was now strong and self-reliant—I was dutifully carrying the burden. What a waste! Today, he still welcomes my love and interest but I'm sure that, on some cosmic plane, he was as delighted as I was when my unnecessary fretting stopped. In effect, the ritual freed us both.

So much of what we carry around is unnecessary or simply stale-dated. Some is on-going, like our children's welfare, but here is the question: does the well-being of our children need to be a dark and troublesome concern, a needling worry that depletes us? Or can we shift this overweening concern in more positive directions—in our mind, in our language, and ultimately in our actions? Maybe it's time you set down the burden of your dear children and allow yourself the simple pleasure of enjoying them more.

Once again, do not delve deeply into past sorrows; and do not tread near lingering fears, dark circumstances, or memories of horrific events. We will tackle those serious haunting shadows later, once you have accumulated more effective magick "swords and daggers" in your arsenal.

Making amends to free your soul

When you examine your heartaches and burdens, you may find issues that could be resolved with a little effort—a dose of humility or an outright apology from you—no matter how long ago it all happened. These are often human-error trespasses, where you played a role in some scenario that went wrong or ended disastrously. You still feel badly about it, embarrassed, or deeply saddened.

What should you do in these cases? Pick up the phone, scrawl a note, send an email, have flowers delivered, or whatever you think is appropriate, without causing the wronged party any stress or discomfort. It won't kill you. Making amends is good soul work. Just don't put undue expectations into the outcome other than finding some measure of closure and inner peace while you are still here on Abred. Remember, the intent is to breathe life into your soul, not to rewrite history.

There isn't one of us walking around on the Great Mother's sweet Earth who hasn't, knowingly or unknowingly, intentionally or unintentionally, wronged someone. It happens. It can't be helped. But do the right thing; make amends and free yourself of regrets. You'll walk the hero's path.

Leave the Cauldron: Sip your Brew

You've steeped in your bath and completed the mental list of all the burdens you carry. It's time to rise from the now-murky waters of the Cauldron of Regeneration. Step out and leave behind all those bad feelings and dread; watch as they slowly spiral down the drain and out into the wild streams and rivers that are the bodily fluids of the Earth Mother. She will purify all those dark feelings. They will disappear by the morning's bright light.

Step into your robe or costume. Blow out the bathroom candle, put the incense in the living room, and make your Witch's Brew in the kitchen. When it's ready, bring a cup out to your chair, light the candle, and place it securely to your North, turn up the music, and sip the perfumed herbal brew. Breathe deeply. Let the Chamomile calm your body and soul, even as the sweet Red Clover and the piquant Sage call to mind the sacred Goddess and the Clan Mothers who planted these same herbs in the ceremonial groves where they worshipped. As you breathe in the steam, you are experiencing an ancient tried-and-true remedy: the taking in of herbal steam water.

> *Steam Waters were important medicinal therapies to our ancestors. In addition to the breathing in of hot herbal combinations formulated for a specific treatment, the healers would collect the droplets of condensed steam from herbal roots, leaves or flowers by the distillation process, and bottle it for later use. I'm sure the effectiveness of Steam Waters was enhanced further by the fact that this is an efficient method of liquid purification, used to produce pure bottled water even today.*

Close your eyes and imagine those ancient times. See yourself comfortable and secure in the familiar presence of the Celtic Clan Mothers—elder women who love, appreciate, and support you. The simple act of conjuring them up in your imagination, and breathing in their calming presence with your steaming tea, will ensure that the sweet love of those energizing spirits attends you tonight. They will help lift the weight from your shoulders and release the pain from your heart.

Now, it's time to flap your wings and take to the sky.

Let the joys of the Unburdening Ceremony begin!

Take a handful of Angelica and Mugwort from the bowl beside the chair and rub them between your palms. Close your eyes and breathe in the fragrance, then toss them high in to the air above so they cascade all over you. Say, "I anoint myself with the Great Mother's gift of cleansing herbs." Repeat if you wish. These herbs have strong psychic properties. The ancients called Mugwort the "Spirit Mother" or "Protective Magick." It was used for everything from nervous disorders, to the robust flavoring of ale, to ridding the body of parasites—an appropriate metaphor for this ritual.

Concentrate on the shimmering light of your Spell of Protection that you cast earlier in the Cauldron. See it glowing brightly all around. Know that you are safe, comfortable, and totally secure.

Stand up. Bow to the north and summon the four Airts as you did in your initiation, welcoming each one with reverence. When you are finished, cast an image of your Golden Power Circle before you. This time, enlarge the ring of light to include the chair behind you. (You will sit later, and it's important to stay within the circle of light at all times.) As you stand within its shimmering glow, say out loud, "Great Mother-Mine, please attend me as I unburden my sweet soul and free my natural spirit. In your name, I invoke the blessed gifts of my own magick. Bless me with Your presence."

Squeeze your left power fist at your side with divine super-strength, feel that surge of blissful energy and shout, "Mother-Mine!" Wait a brief moment to feel the loving presence of your Goddess, then whisper, "Blessed be." Sit back down and relax.

Take a handful of the Bay Leaves. The Bay Laurel Leaf was used ritually to cleanse a new hearth, and was the primary herb used to ensure safe travel. It provides clear vision for any quest, and brings protection and good fortune. Your humble kitchen Bay Leaf has been hiding old secrets, but it will serve you well. Call upon its magical energy now. The Bay Leaf will be your talisman for this ceremony, helping you to see clearly and ushering in the promise of good results. Hold them in your right fist, the leaves pointing straight up, as if you were holding a handful of magical raven feathers.

It's time to consider the first burden you recalled in the Purification Bath. Clearly picture the person, or the issue in question. Imagine this burden sitting behind your neck, stretched across your shoulders. Feel its weight. Now imagine it moves forward until it hovers before you. Nod in recognition and make the gesture of handing over one of your Bay Leaves. Then say firmly but kindly:

> **Burden heavy, no longer mine**
> **Burden carried, too long a time**
> **By fresh resolve, by all my might**
> **Depart in peace. Seek the light**
> **I release thee**
> **Blessed be.**
> **Lighten my soul**
> **Burden, Begone!**

Excellent. It's gone. Released to a better place. Now picture the next burden, feel it weighing heavy on your shoulders and bring it forward. Offer it a Bay Leaf and repeat the spell. In this fashion, bid each and every burden on its way.

For loved ones you are releasing as a burden, you may adjust the last two 'release' lines to say:

Burden I release thee
But love remain. Blessed be.

It is the unnecessary, burdensome aspect of the relationship that you must free yourself from, not their on-going love or any other positive aspects that you are letting go of this magical night.

When you have finished your unburdening, let out several great big sighs and be aware of how much lighter you feel each time you draw a new breath. Roll your shoulders forward and back, and think how much you've lifted from them tonight. Breathe out with a long audible, "Ahhhh."

Stand up again, Bay Leaves in hand, and bid farewell to the North, East, South, and West, thanking them for their attendance. Hold your left Power Fist out before you and say, "Thanks be to the Great Mother, comforter of my heart, for showing me the way. Breathe me strong. Breathe me sure. Breathe fresh life into my unburdened soul. Blessed be."

Release your Golden Power Circle, or "close the circle widdershins (counterclockwise)" as the saying goes. It will disappear. Now clap your hands and punch at the air above your head. Turn up the music and dance. Grab your flagon and take a deep, hearty swig. Remember, our Celtic Clan Mothers knew the importance of celebrating each of life's sweet victories. So should you. Stand tall and straight. You are no longer a sad pack horse, a beast of burden. You are a young colt, kicking up its heels in the sweet spring meadow. Nothing can stop you now. You are free!

Later, when you go to your bed this night, place the Bay Leaves under your pillow to bring a well deserved, restful sleep. And if by chance you should dream, hold on to those dreams, for you may find that they are most significant.

My
Sacred
Place

My
Nemeton

Chapter Four

Find Your Nemeton—
Your Own Sacred Place

Better than an anti-depressant or a stiff drink when you're rattled, it's a "room of your own," to escape to where no one can follow. A little piece of heaven. Celtic mystics called it a "*Nemeton,*" an enchanted healing place. Here on the earthplane, it might be found in a sacred grove of oak trees but, more specifically, the word refers to a natural and beautiful setting in your very own soul. Do you need such a place of retreat when the going gets rough? You can have it. It's a gift from the Goddess. Just reach down, grab the hem of your luminous flowing robes, and follow me in merry measure.

Despite our alienation from nature, an unfortunate by-product of urban life, each of you has a sacred place that exists in your mind as a vestige of comforting memory, or as a necessary invention of your imagination. It is a quiet place in which you may re-connect with the feminine divine. A place to slow your racing pulse and calm your heart and soul—a true haven for psychic healing. With a little effort and concentration, you can rediscover that place.

Maybe it was a place you knew and loved, a beautiful way station on life's journey—somewhere you were truly happy, totally safe, and unconditionally loved. It may be a creaky swing in your grandmother's backyard, a particular seashore from a romantic vacation, or a beach where you wandered as a youth seeking answers that somehow always came. Your Nemeton could be a single room that you loved to be in so much, you still recall every feature—the smell of leather-bound books on a shelf, the lemon-scented furniture polish, or maybe the pleasing sight of dried rose petals in a flared glass bowl, or the swoosh of an old-fashioned ceiling fan. Yes, a special room may well be your Nemeton—your power place.

The ancient Goddess worshippers considered nature to be the sacred body of the Mother Goddess—what is commonly known as Mother Nature. They believed that the natural environment housed powerful spirits and had a personality all of its own. It is a living, breathing, and feeling entity worthy of great honor and respect. Celtic tradition, then, would favor a natural setting as your Nemeton: a lake, a seashore, a meadow, a forest grove, or a place tucked away in the mountains.

If you feel that a place in nature may be most appropriate and powerful as your Nemeton, you can either recall some magical setting from your childhood, or a holiday location you enjoyed so much that the feelings of peace and relaxation lasted long after your return. Or you can imagine a perfect place you only hope to visit one day. It may be a place you've seen in magazines, or in film, or even one you've created in your fertile imagination. It doesn't matter. A Nemeton may be many things, but it's one thing for certain—a comfortable, familiar place where you have a feeling of absolute well-being. A place you could consider "home for your soul."

The Clan Mothers knew well the healing benefits of establishing a Nemeton and passed on this wisdom to their young female students. In the same fashion, through mother-to-daughter, it has made its way down to me. Consider me your uniformed and cheery cosmic travel agent.

Your Personal Itinerary for Travel to Your Nemeton

Cost of this cosmic travel? Absolutely Free.

Date and time of departure? Any time of the day or night.

Port of departure? Any place you chose.

Value gained from your trip? Absolutely Priceless.

What a deal! How can you miss? Your Nemeton promises that much-needed pause from the stresses and occasional chaos of your hectic life. Once you have spent a little time there, you will come back refreshed, renewed, and amazingly calm—ready to pick up the threads of your tumultuous life with the attitude that you can handle anything. Because, of course, you can.

Modern vestiges of the original teachings of our Clan Mothers

It's a shame we don't have Clan Mother classes in every city, town, and village. These older women played a crucial role in teaching young women what to expect from life, how to cope and how to access the Otherworld—when and where they need it. They were reliable, no-nonsense teachers that have no counterpart in our life and times. But all is not lost to you, dear friend. If you look hard enough, you'll find a few women here among us today who still deliver wise counsel and answers to life's great riddles.

One who possesses ancient Clan Mother wisdom is Dr. Clarissa Pinkola-Estes. You are probably familiar with her landmark book, *Women Who Run with the Wolves*. It examines ancient myths and legends of the feminine divine. She uses these legends as beacons to light the sometimes dark and rocky paths of Abred for fellow women travelers. She is an exciting writer, a Jungian and Freudian psychologist, and a marvelous storyteller. Her writings point the way back to your wild instinctive nature. If you give her observations the attention they deserve, you will soon rekindle your own sense of women's traditional "knowing."

I have included *Women Who Run with the Wolves* in the Tinder Box of Sacred Tools to be read as a follow-up exercise to your ritual meditation. It is amazing how many of the legends recounted in the book deal with women descending from Abred to enter the Otherworld, or underworld, in order to learn and to grow. This is why finding, securing, and returning to your Nemeton is one of the basic lessons of self-preservation that the Goddess instructed the Clan Mothers to pass on to you. It is so vitally important to be able to escape from harm's way, to anchor our tattered and torn sailing ship in a safe, calm bay in order to wait out the worst of life's storms.

The Nemeton is an extension of your conscious state, but it is an uncommonly peaceful place. It's a comforting refuge for your body and mind where it is possible to learn and understand spiritual teachings, to talk with your spirit guide, to walk with the Gentle Ones, and to leave the harsh reality of the plane of Abred behind for a short while.

The serious life and death value of having a Nemeton

To the Goddess Clan and other matrilineal tribes around the world, the concept of a Nemeton had an even more serious purpose. It had real "life or death" value then, and it still does today. In the midst of life's worst-case scenarios, the ancients found that having a sacred place in the Otherworld could save your life. How so? By securing your Nemeton as a refuge, you are forearming yourself against life's harshest realities. The ancient Celtic world was a violent and life-threatening place for women of all ages, much as our world is today. In olden times, all young girls were taught practical self-defense skills, and they knew the Nemeton provided an escape hatch which allowed them to separate their soul from their bodies in times of overwhelming fear, physical and/or sexual attack, or even attempted murder.

Some Native American tribes also taught their daughters this life-preserving skill of "slipping from their skin" when physical escape was no longer possible. Like the Celtic Clan Mothers, they knew from generations of experience that developing this psychic ability could mean the difference between succumbing to a horrid death, or having the soul power to survive, despite grave physical injury. Training women to endure calamity, to live on and to heal another day, was their ultimate goal. Survival was supreme.

Victims of violent rape have attested to this kind of mind and body separation, claiming they felt that they actually "went somewhere else" during the physical onslaught and pain. In some cases, it is said, the Clan Mothers had to gather around a woman who had been brutalized, and call to the woman's spirit, coaxing it slowly back in to her body. In Celtic times, rape was not very prevalent since the Clan Mothers had long-ago declared it, along with murder, to be a capital offense. Moreover, their laws declared that it was the victim who stood as judge, and she alone decided the ultimate fate of the rapist—an interesting legal procedure that might be reconsidered in our judicial system today.

But enough of this sad talk of violence and mayhem. Let me surround you with the white light of protection against such a personal tragedy ever happening to you.

> *May I, with the blessing of the Goddess who loves you so, take this moment while we are together, to cast an all pervading light of protection around you, that you—dear reader, dear friend—will never, ever experience the misfortune of such a horrendous crime against your person. Blessed be.*

Soon you will learn to use your personal woman's magick to add another layer of everlasting protection for your spirit. Through meditation, and mastering the trigger action called the **Thumb of Knowledge** that I will teach you, you'll be able to visit your sacred place whenever you need the peace and serenity it affords you. But first, let me tell you a little story.

Bumping into my Nemeton in a darkened bathroom

I first came to know my Nemeton when I experienced that dreaded "end of the rope" feeling that comes when you are absolutely exhausted, but still have to cope with three highly charged, overly energetic children. I wasn't physically well at the time and unfortunately my mother—my own contemporary Clan Mother—was many long miles away.

I lived in the suburbs of Dallas, Texas, and on that particular afternoon the summer heat was harsh and relentless. The temperature was so high, the children would have burned themselves on the metal swing set outside; so everyone was inside, cooled artificially by the overworked air conditioners.

My exhaustion and health problems sapped my dwindling energy and dragged down my spirit. Added to my growing malaise was the realization that my marriage was coming to an end. A bleak picture.

The children were particularly quarrelsome, bickering with each other to the point of tears. All I wanted was a few moments of breathing space, some privacy, some love. I calmed the children with books and treats, then slipped into my ensuite bathroom. Bathrooms are a place of sanctuary for many women. We can momentarily lock the world out, and there's life-giving water—the sacred body fluid of the Goddess. Mine was a windowless half-bath. I sat perched on the toilet lid in the dark and—you guessed it—I sobbed uncontrollably. There seemed no way out. No joy. No peace. No hope. I was beginning to believe the real me had somehow disappeared from the planet. Sound familiar?

Suddenly, something jolted me. A kind of energy shot through me and I sat up straight. I stopped crying and suddenly, there I was, standing at the seashore. No kidding. Had I lost my sanity? I knew I was experiencing some kind of altered state of consciousness. It was nothing short of amazing and it got my full attention. One moment I was the Great Bathroom Weeper, the next I was strolling barefoot along a sandy beach! Instead of wallowing in self-pity, I was spiritually transported.

Looking back, I realize I was in what the Clan Mothers called "the perfect emotional place." My life was in the balance, and I could have gone either way—into mental and physical breakdown; or, as actually happened, into a calming imaginary place, an altered state of mind. Without realizing it, I had chosen the healing help of the Goddess wisdom within me. I was suddenly transported to my Nemeton for the very first time. She had taken my hand and led me gently to it.

No more snivelling. In my mind, I was no longer perched on a toilet seat in a dark half-bath in the suburbs, besieged by dark thoughts. No way. I was now a free spirit, ambling effortlessly along the wide expanse of my private ocean beach. My idea of paradise. Pleasantly barefoot. Leaving a trail of shallow footprints in the velvety sand behind me, each indentation proving that I was "still here," that I "still existed." It was the verification I so desperately needed.

And, as in all subsequent visits to my Nemeton, the tactile sensations were vivid and dramatic. I felt the damp mist from the waves on my face and arms, smelled the salty air and seaweed, and sensed the slight sinking of the sand beneath the weight of each of my footsteps. The light was gentle and easy on the eyes. I stared at the great body of Mother Goddess ocean before me and it gave me the stability my spirit was seeking. The beach was a place of peace and serenity where I began to re-establish faith in myself and hope for my future. This enchanting place calmed me, healed me.

It's amazing where and when spiritual instruction might suddenly be visited upon you. When all seemed lost, I received a spiritual helping hand. The tight muscles around my face and skull relaxed. My rock-hard shoulders dropped back to their normal, comfortable position. All my muscles softened. I breathed out a long sigh of grateful relief and knew, instinctively, that I could and would be able to cope. I had been given the sacred gift of my Nemeton and I've returned to and enjoyed that magical place ever since. So can you.

Preparations for the Nemeton Ceremony

As before, the Tinder Box of Sacred Tools will help you assemble all the materials you'll need to make the ceremony meaningful. If you're using Quick Minute Magick, please pay particular attention to the instructions that follow.

Quick Minute Magick: Finding Your Nemeton Meditation Ritual

If you're using the Quick Minute Magick method, you're probably getting pretty skillful at experiencing the events in your mind and body—feeling the power surges, smelling the sweet aroma of incense and savoring the flavor of the Witch's Brews. Good for you. The mind is a miraculous instrument. Just because you're a busy go-getter doesn't mean you can't do meaningful soul development work. This jiffy method doesn't diminish the effect of the ceremonies and rituals at all. Say to yourself, "Great Mother, thanks be for mind travel."

This Nemeton ceremony is a Ritual Meditation—a form of meditation that is centered in magical ritual enactments for maximum amplification of the spiritual results. You will want to choose a quiet place for this Quick Minute Magick, because it may appear that you've fallen asleep while you "experience" the meditation. That could prove a bit embarrassing on the bus or the subway train. So, try stretching out on a blanket somewhere—a beach would be my choice, but any quiet, private room would be just fine. Remember to cast your Spell of Protection even as you read this, don't forget to make your Power Fist and say, "Mother-Mine" at the appropriate time, and follow the other steps faithfully.

When you are finished, sit back and relax and enjoy the experience of travelling to your Nemeton. At the end of the chapter, you'll find instructions so that you can visit your sacred place any time you choose. It will serve you well. Enjoy. You are powerful and—*wow*—are you one fast spinner of ritual!

The Tinder Box of Sacred Tools is smaller and more compact this time, but the herbs which draw on the visionary powers of the psyche should definitely be included. Also, two semi-precious stones have been added to the ritual to enhance your voyage. Either one will do if you already own one, but two would be even better. If you have neither, simply bring a favored rock that is small enough to hold in your hand.

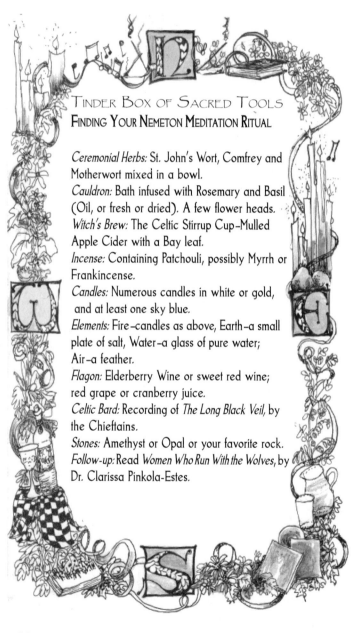

TINDER BOX OF SACRED TOOLS
FINDING YOUR NEMETON MEDITATION RITUAL

Ceremonial Herbs: St. John's Wort, Comfrey and
Motherwort mixed in a bowl.

Cauldron: Bath infused with Rosemary and Basil
(Oil, or fresh or dried). A few flower heads.

Witch's Brew: The Celtic Stirrup Cup–Mulled
Apple Cider with a Bay leaf.

Incense: Containing Patchouli, possibly Myrrh or
Frankincense.

Candles: Numerous candles in white or gold,
and at least one sky blue.

Elements: Fire–candles as above, Earth–a small
plate of salt, Water–a glass of pure water;
Air–a feather.

Flagon: Elderberry Wine or sweet red wine;
red grape or cranberry juice.

Celtic Bard: Recording of *The Long Black Veil,* by
the Chieftains.

Stones: Amethyst or Opal or your favorite rock.

Follow-up: Read *Women Who Run With the Wolves,* by
Dr. Clarissa Pinkola-Estes.

Significance of the Tinder Box of Sacred Tools

In this ritual meditation you will call forth the presence of Briganntia or Brigit, the Celtic Mother Goddess. It will please Her to have more candles than usual since She, in one of her many aspects, is the spirit of the home hearth—the Fire Goddess.

> *Brigit, as the Fire Goddess, was highly revered by the ancient Mothers. Her presence as seen in the roaring flames and wild sparks meant physical warmth, light to work by, and the life-giving sustenance of hot, nutritious food. Women moved easily around the raised central hearths that also served as their natural altars to Her. They spoke with Her, told Her their problems or concerns, praised Her comfort and understanding, and beseeched Her help and protection for family and friends. She was a familiar and comforting daily presence in their cottages. Brigit filled their humble homes and loving hearts with Her motherly concern, approval, and divine blessing.*

Candles: For the color of the candles, I turn to the authority of author and mystic, Patricia Telesco. She is a well-known and highly respected practitioner of folk magick, humbly referring to herself as a 'Kitchen Witch.' She has shared her special talents and magical skills through more than 50 metaphysical books including: *A Charmed Life* and *Goddess in My Pocket* and the more recent book *Exploring Candle Magick—Candle Spells, Charms, Rituals, and Divinations*. Patricia suggests that you include a sky blue candle to symbolize joy, new beginnings, psychic awareness and, specifically for this ceremony, to represent travel magick.

The Goddess Brigit is symbolized by white candles—spirit candles—and by candles of a golden hue. To welcome the Goddess to this ceremony, arrange a tray of six to 10 candles grouped together to symbolize the flaming hearth altar within the Clan Mothers' cottages. This candle energy will help light your way. Although white has always been my choice for ritual and ceremonial power magick, the additional energy brought by the golden candles will enhance the ceremony and focus the energy to spiritual purpose. Thanks be to Patricia Telesco for sharing her wealth of information.

Bard: Your Bard for this journey will be the Chieftains amazing recording, *The Long Black Veil.* I especially recommend the goosebump-raising first cut by Sting, as he sings in Gaelic about the Celts' deep reverence for noble courage in a hero. In this ritual, you are the admirable hero he sings about.

Magick Stones: It would be great to have magical stones present at this ritual. One is the purple Amethyst. It can be in the form of the rough-cut rock, or polished and set in a piece of jewelry. Amethyst is known as a fierce protecting stone that both energizes the owner and acts as a cleansing agent to screen out unwanted energies. It also encourages humor and happiness, two valuable qualities wanted on the inner voyage. For this ritual, it is the Amethyst's power to assist with meditation that will be its most valuable aspect to guide you to your Nemeton.

The other magical stone is the Opal. The dancing firelight found within the stone is a symbol of Brigit. You most likely have one that is set in a ring or brooch. That's fine. Bring it. Opals have long been celebrated for their power to assist on inner journeys, meditations, and astral travel while offering the benefit of calming properties. Either stone will add power to the effectiveness of your meditation experience. Hold one, or both, in your right hand when you cast your Golden Power Circle.

Ceremonial Herbs: For this meditation ritual you'll have a bowl of mixed dry herbs of St. John's Wort and Motherwort to anoint yourself at the beginning of the ritual.

St. Johns' Wort was called Tutsan by the Welsh Celts long before the introduction of saints. It was an effective remedy for injuries and the resulting inflammation before the world was gifted with antibiotics. Spiritually, the Clan Mothers employed the magick of the herb to commune with the fire spirit which is the Goddess. It was also invaluable for dispelling any unwanted presence, to reduce anxiety, and to lift up the spirits. St. John's Wort is currently popular for those very qualities of dispensing with emotional darkness or depression.

Motherwort was indispensable in the birthing room and was used to enhance the flow of mother's milk. The effectiveness of this sacred woman's herb often meant the difference between life or death for a newborn. Named for the Great Mother and all her nurturing qualities, Motherwort promotes inner confidence that your new venture will turn out well.

Altering your state of mind

Unlike the Personal Power Ritual and the Unburdening Ritual, finding your Nemeton is achieved through entering a slightly altered state of mind—a ritual meditation of Celtic origin. Now, don't be leery of shifting to an altered state of consciousness. And don't be scared. You do altered state transitions every day. "I do?" You flash back at me. Yes, you do! When you gaze out the window and daydream, you are in the kind of altered state we are talking about for this ritual meditation. So don't be nervous in the least. You are well prepared to step into another place, and you will do so with as much ease as when you allow your mind to wander into a lovely daydream. Both are effortless; both are natural.

Rapping on the oaken door: Steps of the Nemeton Meditation Ritual

My mother had two expressions whenever she asked me to go into my inner peaceful self for answers. "Sit and find your feet," she would say, meaning to center myself in preparation for any spiritual quest. Or, if she noticed I was particularly nervous or distracted, she'd gently suggest that perhaps it was time to "Rap on the oaken door," which we sometimes did together to begin a ritual meditation or to initiate a spirit channeling.

The wood from the oak tree is highly significant. The traditional three-legged stool, so often used by a Celtic medium to tap out spirit messages "from beyond" was always made of oak. We know that the original Gaelic meaning of Nemeton is really an oak tree grove, a sacred place where Druids, Clan Mothers and, later, dedicated witch covens were known to assemble and worship the Goddess.

The folk magick faery mounds, which are an integral part of the Old Religion, were all characterized as having a charming, round-topped oaken door that opened to their secret world. It was a small portal "betwixt and between" what we know as reality and the Otherworld. Sometimes you could find this mystical entrance door; most times you could not. So, throughout the centuries upon centuries, the oaken door has been the time-honored Celtic spiritual portal to another place, another time, another dimension. And it will serve you, as well. When the time comes, we'll rap three times with determination and confidence upon that stout oaken door, and walk through to another realm where you will be welcomed in the fine old Celtic tradition of generous hospitality.

You've successfully maneuvered two rituals with me so far, and I'd bet that the cumulative experience has been uplifting and broadening. First, you mastered how to lock-in your Personal Magick and Power. You learned the simple physical trigger of your left Power Fist that summons all the incredibly strong magick that is your base, that is the bliss of your Goddess within. Secondly, we went through the process of clearing the psychic decks—identifying your burdens, wishing them a fond farewell, and freeing up your soul for more positive endeavors.

This ceremony has similar elements to the other two, albeit with specialized herbs and other sacred tools. Ritual is just that—the symbolic and heartfelt repetition of small acts to accomplish a specific goal. In this ritual meditation ceremony, you'll learn the process of finding your own path and further customizing your woman's magick. Through the regular use of this ritual meditation, you'll "find your feet" and they'll take you to your sacred Nemeton, whenever you need it.

Begin your travel adventure to your Nemeton

Here are the details of your ritual meditation. Make haste. It's time to go. Blessed be your spiritual journey, dear friend.

First, as always, take a purification bath with a white candle burning safely near the tub. Light the incense containing Patchouli or, if possible, Myrrh or Frankincense and watch its perfumed smoke swirl upward like a sweet prayer. Your bath is infused with the herbs Rosemary and Basil. Basil, as you know, serves as a support for novices and as a release for any pent-up fears or visions. It represents the initial magical act of stepping outside yourself. Rosemary can be found at the grocery store. Swish the fresh needle-like stalks around in your bath, or crush the fresh or dried herb between your fingers and inhale the heady, aromatic oil. This addition of the oil of Rosemary to your Cauldron will regenerate your body, soothe aching limbs and act as a stimulant to push away any trace of nervous exhaustion. Its spiritual qualities enhance memory and will help you sort through your memory bank for the perfect cosmic destination to serve as your magical Nemeton.

Rosemary and Basil used ritually in combination means the numinous powers of these herbs are further intensified. They are excellent support herbs as you venture down any new spiritual path. The blending of their herbal oils will ensure you are infused with courage and strength of purpose, and that you are spiritually purified and ready for this meditation ritual.

As you lower yourself into the steaming bath that is your Cauldron of Inspiration and Regeneration, you will begin to experience the Cauldron's blessings. Let out a long sigh of joy as you relax fully and completely into its soothing warmth and fragrance. You are being regenerated physically and emotionally. Its calming waters offer you the inspiration to accomplish what lies ahead. Cast the Spell of Protection around your body and take a moment to think about the Cauldron in which you recline this very moment.

Brigit, the Goddess of Fire, was mistress of the original Cauldron. It was said to bubble with restorative herbs, flowers, and plants that bestowed powers of eloquence, inspiration, prophesy and song on all who breathed of its steam. Breathe in the fragrance of the blessed Basil and the pungent Rosemary, and luxuriate at the sight of the floating, bobbing flower heads. The power of the feminine divine is all encompassing, all enduring. She comes again after years shrouded in disguises, hidden by the shadows of violent persecutions. She comes to comfort you.

It is now time to recall those places that might include the one most comfortable and beloved destination to serve as your sacred Nemeton. In your search, you may have to weigh a number of real places against some make-believe ones. Or perhaps, as in my instant travel to the seashore, you will know instinctively where you feel happiest.

What are the basic prerequisites for labeling a place as your Nemeton? It must have an aura of peace and joy, of gentle bliss like your collection of Power Magick memories. Another requirement is that your sacred place make you feel uplifted as well as secure and safe. My mother used to say—here I go again, but she *was* one of my Clan Mothers—that you should feel "safe as a wee cricket in the Goddess' apron pocket." If you still have trouble choosing a place, swish your branch of Rosemary around the Cauldron waters. The herbs will help you isolate and confirm the exact location of your sacred place. Now that you've decided on the setting for your Nemeton, we will do a ritual meditation and take you there to claim it.

Step out of your bath and say a heartfelt "Thanks be" to the herbs and flowers that assisted you on this search. Dry briskly to stir up the blood energy, and put on your magical costume. (It's a good idea to have a special piece of clothing that you use each and every time you do a ceremony. The same ceremonial dress will serve two purposes: slipping it on will signal to your psyche that you have begun your spiritual journey; and it will usher in feelings of anticipation that will magnify and intensify the extent of your personal magick.)

Blow out the bath candle and take the incense to the living room so it too will be filled with the magical smoke. Go to the kitchen and brew up your Witch's Brew which is named in the old Celtic tradition—the Stirrup Cup.

"*What's a Stirrup Cup?*" Well, it was traditional for the Clan Mothers to present a warm drink to anyone in the tribe who was embarking on a journey. The traveler had to be in the saddle, ready to go, before the Stirrup Cup was ceremoniously handed up to them. The recipient would drink it as an omen of good fortune and as protection for both heart and limb.

You could say it was a form of medieval travel insurance. Drinking the potion of blessed herbs was known to guarantee a safe and successful trip. After sipping from the Stirrup Cup, the traveler would pull off their left boot (the sacred and profane side of their spirit) and an Elder would solemnly place a Bay Leaf in the bottom of the boot for further luck and safety. Once the ceremony was officially over, the traveler would depart, kicking his horse up to speed as friends cheered and hooted, banged iron pots, and threw fresh flowers and herbs. Yapping dogs and small children followed in hot pursuit for as long as they could keep up. What a joyous, vibrant way to garner bushels of good energy at the start of a lengthy journey!

To make your own Stirrup Cup, add slightly warmed apple cider or apple juice to a mug and stir with a Bay Laurel Leaf; then, discard the leaf and sip your sacred drink. There. 'Tis assured. The Clan Mothers bless you. Only good things will come on this special soul journey to your Nemeton.

You may finish your drink in the living room while you listen to your bard, Sting, as he sings to you in the ancient Gaelic language—the language of the early Celts. It is a sound from another time when music was sung under the protective smile of the Mother Goddess, and it tells the story of a tribe's adoration and reverence for the courage of a Celtic hero. Now imagine that Sting sings to you, because he does. You drink an ancient potion, he sings in the ancient language, and you are both transported to another time and place when the Goddess was our deity and each woman was exalted as an image of the Goddess incarnate. So you are again, this very evening.

Then set the Stirrup Cup down near your bowl of ceremonial herbs. Light the tray of candles and place it to your north. Make sure it's steady and won't fall over, no matter how much you dance.

If you need your memory refreshed at this point, I recommend that you turn back and quickly review the steps from the previous rituals you have already completed. Then enact the basic rites: welcome the Airts, cast your Golden Circle, make your Power Fist, and call up the energy of the Goddess. Once all is in place, sit back down and reach into the bowl of ceremonial herbs (St. John's Wort and Motherwort). Rub them between your palms and throw a handful or two high above you so they drift back down, covering your hair, shoulders, and arms. You are ready to begin your meditation.

The ritual meditation in Celtic tradition

You may wish to read through this section in advance and make note of the steps, so you don't need this book to guide you throughout the process. Please keep in mind that it is important to carry out this meditation ritual with no real effort expended. In other words—don't try too hard. Relax, and flow with it. It's a natural and comfortable journey that needs no effort on your part except enjoyment.

If you've never meditated before, or are a little nervous and find it hard to "let go," do the following easy exercise first, so that you will realize this most important fact: **You are always in total control.** Regardless of where your spirit takes you, you can return in an instant to this room, this chair, this reality. Go ahead and test it. Close your eyes. Say out loud to the forces of love and good, "I am in total and complete control. I can open my eyes in a flash and be right back here in my chair." Now, open your baby blues and study the room. Nothing has changed. You haven't changed. You're the master of this ship. Indeed, you can be safely back in your chair anytime, or as many times as you wish, during your meditation. Does that comfort you? There's no hocus-pocus going on here, no surrendering of your personal control. The meditation is powered by your inner self, and it is *totally* protective of you. So, be serene. Be confident. You're in good hands—your very own.

Ready to fly

Be sure your feet are flat on the floor and your spine is straight, but relaxed. Put the magical Opal, Amethyst, or your trusty rock on your lap, and place your hands on the arms of the chair. Close your eyes and take three deep breaths. As you breathe in through your nose, imagine the air is full of fragments of yellow light, like tiny yellow clouds. Inhale to the count of three (that magical number of our Clan Mothers); hold it for three counts; then exhale through your mouth slowly, again to the count of three. As before, in the relaxing process, imagine you are exhaling black, sooty air on the first count; dirty grey air with the second healing count; and finally, clear pure air by the third count as you cleanse your body of past dark influences and worries. Repeat two more times. You are ready.

Take a few more breaths if you feel the need. Let your body relax totally. Your legs are warm and heavy; your torso is comfortable and calm. Sink back into the upholstery. Your shoulders drop; your neck and head relax.

You may now dictate how long you will be in a meditative trance. Say, for example, "I am going to my sacred place, my own tranquil Nemeton. I will be gone for 15 minutes or less."

Now, imagine that you are standing before yourself, while you still sit in the chair. See yourself sitting comfortably in the chair. Then, switch places, and watch yourself standing before the chair. This standing image of you turns and walks away. Go along with her. You climb a few stairs and reach a landing where there is a door.

Envision an ancient Celtic portal before you. It is the legendary and much-loved great oaken door. Picture it clearly before you and admire it for a moment. Study it. They don't do workmanship like that anymore, do they? It's sturdy and strong and will last for a good long time to come. This old door is in excellent condition, its dark wood polished to a soft, glowing patina. It has recessed panels and the top of the door is gently rounded. It's quite charming, isn't it?

Look carefully at the handle. It can be anything you want. Is it old polished brass? Maybe it's an iron handle, forged by a blacksmith's hand and covered with Celtic animal figures inscribed in the metal. Or maybe your door handle is simply a polished curve of oak, worn smooth by centuries of use. It is your mystical oaken door, finish it any way that appeals to you.

The door represents all that is solid and reliable. It was lovingly crafted from a slab of rough, raw wood. It was sawed and shaped with sharp tools that gouged out the unnecessary bits to reveal its artful design. Your door was drilled and pegged and joined, then finally rubbed all over with coarse and fine sandpaper until it fairly shone. Over the years it has been battered and banged about. Now it is weathered and marked, but it is beautiful—one of a kind. It has endured, as you have. You are that same sturdy work of art. You are a beautiful soul.

You see, this faery mound door is a mirror of your being. Knock. Go ahead. Give it three hard, measured raps. The Forces of Good know you are coming and they welcome you. Reach for the handle. Push it easily open. Pass through and say, "Thanks be."

Imagine a down flight of time-worn stairs before you. Look at your bare feet. Wiggle your toes. Step down, watching your foot as you place it on the first stair tread. This will be the first of 10 stair steps. Your flight of stairs can be made of wood or metal or even rough-cut stone, like mine, which are set in to the side of a gently sloping hill that leads down to my beach. Any type of stair will do, just be aware of each one and concentrate on how the steps feel when your foot lands on them. Are they smooth and warm? Cool to the touch? Cushy soft and carpeted with moss? Look at your bare foot and experience the feel of the first stair tread as you say, "One. I am going deeper." See the next stair before you and watch your foot as it moves with great confidence and surety down upon it. Say, "Two. I am going deeper to my Nemeton." Repeat to the number 10. I guarantee that you will feel very relaxed, very calm. You feel great. You are enjoying this adventure.

At the bottom of the stairs, step out on to grass, sand, or stone. Your choice. Pause and look around. There it is before you, just a short walk in front of you. Your sacred place. Your Nemeton.

Allow yourself a smile while you study the details. Are there trees? What kind? How many? Note the temperature of the air and the quality of the light. Is there a body of water nearby? Step into your sacred place. There will be a bench or a seat to sit on that feels just right. Sit down and listen for sounds. Listen hard, for some are not readily discernible at first. Do you hear the gentle lapping of waves, or a distant bird's song or the dry rustle of the breeze in the leaves above? Smell the fragrant air and feel the warmth of the sun on your arms, your face. Breathe in the tangible peace of your sacred place. Breathe deeply and allow yourself the luxury of just being—no pressures, no expectations, nothing to be resolved. Be part of the here and now of your Nemeton. It is beautiful because you have created it. This is your haven from now on, forever after.

Move around in your space, if you like. Explore. Enjoy. Or simply sit and drink it all in. Give in to the gentle feeling of well-being and happiness. No one and nothing can disturb your joy when you are in your Nemeton.

Stay as long as you wish. You've already predetermined how long you will be in your meditation, so don't worry for a moment about time passing. When you are ready to go, just retrace your steps. Don't fret that your Nemeton will disappear, that you will lose it. It is always there waiting patiently for your return. And there's no pressure on you to return at any particular time. Any time is perfect. Everything is perfect. You are perfect.

As you ascend your staircase, simply count out the numbers of each stair from 10 back up to one. You may find that you happily swing your arms, or dash up the last several steps, shouting out the numbers like a child in a hurry. At the top you'll find your Celtic portal, your oaken door. Fling it open and step through. Walk over to where you are sitting quietly in your chair, and simply sit back down. Plunk. Spirit and body are one again. Open your eyes and take a deep breath. You feel refreshed, maybe even a bit giddy. You're ready to take on anything and anyone.

Thumb of Knowledge trigger

But wait, beautiful soul. There is one important step still left to do on this joyous occasion of the first visit to your Nemeton. You have to set up a trigger mechanism that will allow you to visit your sacred place in an instant, any time you wish. It is called the Thumb of Knowledge and it is a ritual so tried and true, so steeped in ancient tradition, that even the Clan Mothers used it thousands of years ago. It originates in faery folklore from the forgotten mists of time, yet it is a most effective sacred tool. Now it is yours to use. Here's how:

Put your magical stones aside and stand up, big and tall. Lift your left hand and make your Power Fist to reinforce the magick in this triggering. Say, "Mother-Mine," in a good strong voice. Now open your Power Fist and bring your left hand up to your mouth. Press your thumb firmly against your top front teeth, adding a little pressure, so you feel it but it doesn't hurt. Concentrate and draw up the image of your lovely Nemeton for a brief moment while your thumb rests against your teeth. Got it? Good. Close your eyes and say, as a strong statement of fact, "Nemeton-Mine." It is done. You've established a physical trigger. Whenever you press that thumb to your teeth and say those two words, it will all come back, every delicious detail. Your spirit will fly to your Nemeton instantly. Now, aren't you the maker of small miracles? You are. Believe it.

Lower your hand. As in other ceremonies, thank the Goddess for the blessing of this gift and for Her attendance of you. Thank and release the four Airts. Hold your Power Fist straight up in front of you and pledge to use your power only for the good. Open your circle by imagining that it disappears counter-clockwise. Your Ritual is finished. Clap your hands up over your head. Yes! Another great success. You are getting stronger every day. Dance and jump about like a school child who is struck with the joy of simple movement. Start the music but turn it up, turn it higher this time. Sing, Sting, sing! Reach for your Flagon of Elderberry wine or juice and take a good healthy slug in celebration. The hard work is done. Good, successful soul work.

Congratulations, dear friend! You just secured a piece of promised land for yourself. A bit of paradise. A lovely real estate property of the soul. And believe me, your Nemeton will serve you well. Whenever the pressure is on, use your Thumb of Knowledge trigger and in one fell swoop you'll be back in your own specially-tailored paradise. Whenever you feel down or depressed or badly-done-to, or if you simply need a break, go to your Nemeton and restore your spiritual and emotional balance. You can travel there through your full meditation as we did today (and I'd recommend that you do the full meditation a few more times until the journey is smooth and automatic); or you may use your clever little trigger to return in a flash, no matter where you are at the time.

Legendary history of the Thumb of Knowledge

Where did the proverbial Thumb of Knowledge come from, and what mysteries did the Clan Mothers tell about this psychic trigger? Celtic mystics and diviners are known to have used it as their device to bring forth supernatural visions. Whenever a Clan Mother needed to divine the future or to get added assistance with a tribal problem, she would press her thumb to her teeth for inspiration and for wise and knowing solutions.

Clear references to the thumb are found in the Irish legend of Finn MacCoul. It is said that Finn injured his thumb when leaving the faery mound after a night of joyful and raucous partying. He planned to leave just before morning light, so he wouldn't be caught there forever; but in his haste, he let the oaken door slam hard and caught his thumb in the door jamb. Ow! So what did he do? Exactly what you would do—he put his sore thumb in his mouth and sucked on it. But when he touched his teeth with the swollen thumb, he was astonished to discover that he had the gift that the Irish still call the "second sight." He had knowledge of the spirits and an ability to commune with them. Somehow, he had developed an understanding of the doings of the mysterious Otherworld and was able to divine the future. And every time he touched his thumb to his teeth, he instantly conjured up his gift of the "sight"—that sacred and numinous knowledge of the beyond. He called it his Thumb of Knowledge.

The wise and astute Clan Mothers of the Goddess found that the Thumb of Knowledge always transported them to the place of 'knowing' that provided reliable answers to their questions. They, in turn, taught all young women the secret, just as I've taught you. It's one of those ancient "women's mysteries" or "women's secrets" that have been around to serve us since the beginning of time.

Stones under your bed

Later tonight, take your Opal, Amethyst, or favorite rock you used in your ritual meditation and slide it under your bed, so that you may be visited by comforting dreams. Dreams that will fill you with confidence and a peaceful heart when you wake again to the morning light. And just before you get out of bed, touch your thumb to your teeth, close your eyes, and allow yourself to travel back for a brief visit to your Nemeton. It is one of the many gifts the Goddess grants to you.

Making the magick of your Nemeton work for you

There are so many situations in which you could benefit from a few stolen moments away from reality, to regroup from the pressures of relationships, or to relieve the stresses of the workplace. By accessing your Nemeton, on a daily basis if you need to, you can turn things around and make them better or easier to handle. Let's look at the workplace, for example.

Unfortunately, the workplace is often not a pleasant, rewarding, or even a sustaining place. If you are in a job that is unfulfilling, or if you expend emotional energy battling office pettiness and backbiting, or even if you are experiencing any kind of career disappointment, you can use a quick visit to your Nemeton. It will give you the break you need to recharge, to renew, or simply to buoy up your emotional strength to get through the difficult times, unscathed.

Here's what you do. Just slip away from your desk or work station and lock the door of a bathroom stall for a moment of privacy. Sit and relax. Make your Power Fist, say "Mother-Mine" and feel the energy fill your body. Then open your fist and press your left thumb against your front teeth. Say: "Nemeton-Mine" and imagine yourself in your special place. Relax. Stay for a refreshing moment or two. Then flash open your eyes and stand up. Throw back your shoulders and step out of your cubicle re-energized and renewed.

It works! You can take my word for this, because I've done it. Many times. I can give you my personal assurance, an iron-clad cosmic guarantee, that you'll emerge a different person, confident, self-assured, and able to take on the world with compassion and love. In those few brief moments, you just reminded yourself that you are divine. Ha! Look at you! You're a truly skilled and knowing Daughter of the Clan of the Goddess.

Meet
Your Spirit
Guide

Chapter Five

Help From the Otherworld—Meet Your Spirit Guide

Celtic Clan Mothers referred to them as "the Old Ones." You may already know them in your life as your guardian angel, or your special friend—the one who whispers good advice in your ear. Surely you've felt that unseen presence at one time or another. The Goddess force, the feminine divine, provides this nurturing spiritual care from the Otherworld to stay beside you, and to love and protect you. Maybe you already have a name for your Spirit Guide, one that you conjured up in your childhood when you pretended to play with an invisible friend. Or, as an adult, you may have felt a moment of warm, reassuring comfort in the midst of a personal crisis even though no one was visibly there. Well, someone was there, and that little "friend" was very real—it was your contact with the Otherworld, your first contact with your Spirit Guide.

Sometimes guides are people who have lived before and have now evolved to a higher dimension. They have been selected to love and guide you—*only you*—on this hazardous journey through Abred. Other times, they are entities or angels who "know all" from their high vantage point, and watch over you day and night. Always dedicated. Ever devoted.

How do you come to know your guide personally? I'll teach you the skill of channeling through ritual mediation techniques, similar to the one you just learned. By using these learned techniques and good intent, along with the blessing of the Goddess, you'll come to know your guide intimately. To walk with them. To talk with them. You may even learn something of their past lives and background, and how it may mysteriously overlap with your own experiences or special interests.

You will add the power of your Spirit Guide (or guides) to your arsenal of Personal Power, your magick. This helper from the Otherworld will keep you from harm, show you the way when times are dark, and someday greet you on the other side when you pass through the river and into the spirit world. You will never again feel alone in the world with your spirit helper at your side.

Your life is crowded with a host of heavenly helpers

Did I just say that you'd never be alone? That makes me laugh, because it's definitely the understatement of the century. If you had a pair of fancy science fiction goggles to make beings from another plane visible to the naked eye, I'd suggest you put them on right now. You don't know it, and you probably never even suspected it, but you are presently and always surrounded by beings and entities—loving, deeply devoted souls from the other side. You'd see an entire roomful, and they are all there for you.

The Clan Mothers believed their pets had the ability to see the spirits, so if your dog or cat or the budgie over there in its cage could talk, they'd gladly tell how many helping spirits attend you. There's actually a small mob of them. You'd begin to feel just like a famous rock star—a Britney Spears type—with a huge and varied "star entourage." And it really isn't all that different. When you think of the Britney Spears example, isn't every person who travels with her there for a good reason? They're all hand-picked for particular talents or specialties so that when she steps on stage, she looks and feels her absolute best—her diva best.

"How does this celebrity stuff relate to me?" Well, entourages aren't the exclusive domain of flashy rock stars. No, indeed! You, my dear friend, have one of your own. It's true! Your spiritual entourage may be invisible to the eye, but it's there. And rest assured, it is composed of the finest professionals—soul-work specialists—chosen to work exclusively on your behalf. They are there to encourage and comfort you; to cheer you on through all the small and major theatrics of your very important life.

If your confidence needs boosting, just remember that your assembled entourage is better than anything money can buy. It is priceless. Every one of the spirits, angels, ancestors, and entities that surrounds you, loves you deeply and unconditionally. You are not only divine, you are a diva in your own right. You have the ability to be every bit as good at anything you set your heart to, just as Britney is at charming the media and pleasing her multitude of fans.

Universal sweet news: You are never alone

A very spiritual, Lakota-Sioux artist friend of mine told me of a lesson she had learned as a child, and recently passed on to her daughter—the Lakota people are "never alone." She said it was important for her teenager to be aware, as she struggled with being a minority in the white man's system, that she was never abandoned, never without support. She told her daughter that if she sat quietly to contemplate the meaning of this rocky road called life, her ancestors would be there with her. These helpers and wise sages from beyond would attend, and their very presence would bring good counsel and serene consolation.

I was delighted. Why? Because the Celtic Clan Mothers taught the exact same thing. I learned at my mother's knee that I had many kindly spirits by my side—I just had to ask for their assistance or be open to their good advice. By asking, I would receive the exact help I needed to figure things out, and it would come to me at the perfect time. I know, too, that in your woman's heart, you sense this spiritual truth—you are never really alone.

I was further amazed when my mother said that the Old Way believed each human was assigned at least seven spirit guides within a lifetime. Seven! One or two were referred to as "main guides," the top grade assignment, I would guess. She explained that main guides often represent major parts of your personality, or are reflections of your soul. They stay at your side throughout your entire life, from birth to death. Other spirit helpers, the specialists in your heavenly entourage, are called in from time to time to guide you through certain segments of your education.

The role of the other Spirit Guides assigned to you

My wise mother, in answer to my hundreds of questions, patiently explained that in addition to our main guides, other Spirit Guides step forward at specific times and in a variety of situations that arise during life's journey. One such guide might appear to bolster your confidence after a grand and terrible disappointment, or an unexpected setback. Another might be that stern voice in your ear, insisting you stop feeling sorry for yourself, that you get up out of bed, and get on with the job.

A Spirit Guide can sweep in like a professional coach to oversee a much-needed comeback. They'll work with you, teaching you the first baby steps back into the essential but sometimes terrifying act of living, breathing, and even loving again. They would be there to lean against when you were too tired to go on, and they'd holler and cheer as you rallied your deep inner courage and moved tentatively forward. You've been through that, haven't you! And, like petite Britney Spears, you too have bodyguards, gentle giants whose very presence give you the burst of inner confidence needed to ease you out of situations where you have stumbled into possible physical danger. Britney's impressively large bodyguards have counterparts on your own cosmic team as well.

Some guides have special technical, intellectual, spiritual, or social skills that will give you the benefit of very practical experience when you most need it. They are spiritual tutors who may be speech writers or public speakers, inventors, or simply spirits with a special talent in a specialization you are just entering. Or they may be a delightful comic who reminds you to laugh, to dance, or to play childish pranks—life's to be enjoyed, after all. The possibilities are endless.

Just be confident, if you are entering a new period in your life or beginning a new vocation or profession, that you will be provided with a special helper to call on for that phase of your journey. A helper who knows "that of which they speak." They will offer advice and steer your thoughts in directions you can count on to be right. Communication with your guides is an invaluable tool for success in any laudable endeavor.

"Wait a minute. How many spirit guides do I have?" Hold up your hand and tick them off on your fingers. What did the Clan Mothers say? Seven—at least seven—kindly Spirit Guides to care for you. And that is a great deal of help from beyond, wouldn't you say? But, of course, there are even more helpers. Yes, there are. And I believe that deep down you may sense

this to be true. Why? Because at times in your life you have felt that you were being guided or watched over, or saved from harm's way by someone—a certain "someone" you knew while they were on Earth, right? You betcha. And your intuition was bang on.

Your Spirit Ancestors attend you

So, dear friend, it turns out you know so much more about spirituality than you realized. Yes, there are Spirit Ancestors, ones you knew intimately or through family stories. Ancestors with human faces you can picture in your mind's eye or look up in a musty old photograph album. These particular spirits are your beloved and most treasured ancestors. In many cases they are women who have passed on to the other side: a grandmother or two; a favorite aunt; a cousin; or maybe even your own dearly-departed and beloved mother. If she is no longer on Abred, I am truly sorry, for there is nothing even close to the all-encompassing, soul nourishing love of a good mother. Yet, in your heart of hearts, you know she is still with you. You feel her presence sometimes, feel her near you. Or a sharp, clear memory may burst into your conscious thoughts, and in those few precious moments you are together again. And do you know what, my clever fey friend? Your feelings are undeniably, absolutely accurate.

And let's not forget the good men you've been blessed to know and love. Your ancestors may include the spirit of a kind and loving grandfather who took you on his knee and told you stories; or maybe he was fierce and everyone feared him—except you—because you had a special understanding. A grandfather of your heart. Perhaps the spirit of a generous and affectionate father hovers close by, constantly reminding you how great you are; or it may be an amusing and generous uncle; or a particularly charming brother; or even a cousin you still miss dearly. Each and every one of these beautiful men was an influence in your life in loving and caring ways.

They are the warmly remembered male relatives who believed in you; who said you could accomplish anything you set your mind to—"just reach out and grab what you desire." Excellent advice. They were men who teased you gently, which is a Celtic sign of great affection. The sort of teasing that showed their love for you to everyone watching. These lovely souls are your Spirit Ancestors. You know exactly who they are. As in life, they still care for and about you. Lucky, lucky you.

And there are others—special friends who have gone before you, or neighbors with whom you shared a bond or special fondness. These spirits are more likely to drop in and out of your memory. They may come to sit vigil with you in solemn or quiet times; or they may appear to share in your gayest, brightest times—just as they once did. Recalling them may remind you to take heed of some rich advice they gave you years ago. Or you may choose to copy one of their good traits, to be more outgoing, or maybe more tolerant. Whatever little bit of fun, frivolity, or wisdom they shared with you in their lifetimes can still return to guide you.

Remember this important axiom for any loved ones who are now on the spirit side:

> *When you remember your departed loved ones, when you bring them to mind, they are there in spirit form with you. If you think of them; they are there. It is a simple and beautiful fact the Clan Mothers taught, and it will bring both comfort and joy to you while you travel here on Abred.*

Meeting my own guardian angel

Wait! I'm still not finished counting. There's your guardian angel, and if you think you know who that may be, trust your instincts. If you believe your great-grandmother is your guardian angel; well, frankly, she is. And if there's someone in history you particularly relate to and wonder sometimes if they've become your guardian angel, I'm here to tell you—they have! Isn't that neat?

Let me tell you about meeting my own guardian angel. My father's brother, Uncle Joe, died as an infant but his memory, brief as it was, was kept alive for me. When I was just a child of eight or nine, I had a vivid dream that I still remember so clearly...

Dear friend, please make a quick note of this: Do you have a vivid dream about someone on the other side that you remember still, no matter how many years ago they passed over? (Nightmares don't count here.) If you do, then look on that dream differently now, for it was more than a simple dream—it was actually a visitation. A spirit visitation. A lovely soul-gift from the beyond.

...back to my own visitation. My Uncle Joe and I were walking down the boulevard on my street, hand-in-hand. He was very tall with white hair, and he was dressed all in white—something akin to a cosmic version of the Man from Glad (who hadn't yet been dreamed up by the advertising executives). I was full of peace and a quiet kind of happiness as we walked along, gabbing away. Even in the midst of the dream,

I had a feeling that this was an important meeting. Finally, I asked him where his wings were—a fair question from a kid meeting her guardian angel for the first time, don't you think? Instantly, he had this great set of white feather wings that almost touched the ground—angel wings—growing out of the back of his neatly tailored, white suit coat. "You are really into the trappings, aren't you?" he teased in a kindly voice. Young as I was, I caught the joke and laughed right along with him. He was right. And, where the cosmos is concerned, I'm still "into the trappings."

Uncle Joe told me a few comforting things about my life and my future that made sense at the time. Then he told me about the work he does on the other side. I've learned many spirits have special skills in addition to guiding human souls, and my Uncle Joe is a sort of cosmic veterinarian who takes care of animals. He said I should remember to call on him whenever I saw an animal in fear or pain, for he had the ability to attend the gentle soul and take away its pain. I've made that request many times over the years, and it has always worked; the injured animal, wild or domesticated, is calmed considerably after I ask for my Uncle Joe's help. (By the way, you too can call on him to relieve an animal's suffering, any time the need arises.)

The morning after my dream, I related every fine detail of the visitation to my mother at the breakfast table. I asked, "Do you think Uncle Joe is my guardian angel?" She raised one eyebrow and asked me back, "Do *you* think he is?" I nodded emphatically, "Yes, I do!" She smiled at me as she passed the strawberry jam, and said softly, "Then he is."

So if you wonder whether someone you knew, loved, or admired is watching over you from the Otherworld and protecting you like a guardian angel—have faith in your intuition. The Clan Mothers would simply say: "Believe it." It's that easy.

Entities: What are they and where do they fit in?

An entity is a spiritual term that is often bandied about, especially in the New Age movement. But to most of us 'entity' is a vague term that is seldom, if ever, clarified. "What are they?" You ask yourself. "Should I be afraid of them? Do I have one, or more? What does all this mean?"

No doubt, like most of us, you've been unduly and negatively influenced by horror movies and science fiction flights-of-fancy. You've been exposed to cinematic sleight-of-hand and ever-improving special effects. Some actor will whisper that there is a "strange entity" in the hallway and we are treated to the image of a diaphanous, floating ghost that uncurls long, see-through fingers with sharp nails. It grimaces, exposing grotesque canine teeth that grow longer and more lethal-looking by the moment. That can be entertaining, and it does get the adrenaline pumping, but as an example of an entity: it's all wrong.

So what are entities, and where do they fit in your heavenly entourage? Entities are extremely positive in nature. They come directly from the very highest planes of spiritual development— the area of complete enlightenment. You can be comfortably at ease with any entities assigned to aid you here on Abred.

"Come on, C.C., what are they, really?" The reason they are seldom explained is because it is difficult to do so, but I'll try. Entities may be manifest as a number of different things, or images. In essence, they are bits and pieces of highly developed and loving wisdom; scraps of endearing love and of enduring cosmic intelligence. They are present at sunrises and sunsets, in shimmering rainbows, and they are especially evident during the *aurora borealis*, that cosmic light show known as the "northern lights." The beauty in nature has many components indicative of these forces of good. Just remember, whatever form they do take, they are always your friends. Friends

from another place and time too complex to understand in our dimension, but important to the success of your present journey on the earthplane. They will flit in and out of your life as needed, bringing bushels of positive, loving energy. And that is a very good thing.

How to banish pesky lesser beings should they drift in

Now, I have to admit there are what I would call "lesser beings." They are less developed, temporarily lost souls who are simply looking for a place, a home. These are not entities. The lesser beings are simply stuck in a spiritual limbo; they are lost and, most likely, a bit frightened by their present situation. Scaring the pants off a human, if they are able to do so, must make them feel a bit alive, don't you think? But if it so happens that you sense the uncomfortable presence of one of these lesser beings—if you feel their darker, brooding presence—you can remedy the situation in a flash. You have the ability to banish them.

Simply make your Power Fist to summon up your woman's magick, and cast a Spell of Protection around yourself and any others with you. Then get bossy. That's right. Tell that presence, whoever they are, to: "leave—go to the light," or, "go home." Say it softly and kindly, but firmly. They will obey. They always do. Or, you may wish to ask your Spirit Guide to take this presence home and be confident they will instantly do so. Then say, "Go in peace, friend." And they will, believe me, each and every time.

Here's another trick. If you are all alone and still feel a bit shaky after banishing the troublesome being—sing. That's right, sing anything you want: hymns, pop songs, silly childhood ditties. Those beings absolutely **hate** song. It'll send them packing—even if you do sing in tune!

By sending them "to the light," or having your guide lead them there, it is even possible that you may be doing some unfortunate, drifting soul a very great and powerful favor. Your simple action may direct them on their way to the Otherworld. At the very least, they will leave you and your loved ones alone.

You are a star of your own celebrity entourage: Enjoy!

I respectfully offer you the gift of knowing your spiritual entourage. Think about who they are in your life. Some you already know. You have a guardian angel to enfold you in the safety of his or her soft wings; two main Spirit Guides who have taken the lofty assignment as your helpmates throughout the up and down adventure here on Earth; a host of other devoted spirit guides; a chorus of loving ancestors and special friends who have gone before and watch out for you in every way; and, lastly, a sparkling bunch of wise and truly enlightened entities, shoring you up with amazing wisdom exactly when you need it. And best of all, your personal entourage has only one focused goal in mind, day and night, and that is **you**.

The path to meeting your main Spirit Guide

Well, we've rounded up all the usual suspects, but we're a little short on names, faces and backgrounds, aren't we? I guess you'd like to get to know your spirit guides a little better.

I'll show you the way. But hang on tight, for you are about to experience something that will change your life forever. You are about to meet one of your dearest friends—your main Spirit Guide (or Guides). Your main Spirit Guides are the ones who know you best. They are aware of all the good, and the not-so-good, and the in-between that is the real you, and the real me—yet they still love us dearly. Unconditionally and completely. So come meet these heavenly souls. And won't that be fine?

A number of different ways to channel your Spirit Guide

Yikes! Just the word "channel" is enough to send most women running in the opposite direction. Isn't that a special gift that telephone psychics and a few television personalities have at their disposal? *"How can I channel? I'm new at this, I just want to meet my Spirit Guide,"* you tell me in no uncertain terms.

Well, you'll be pleasantly surprised to learn that most channelers say the trance plane where they pick up their vibrations isn't nearly as deep as the trance you created in our last mediation together—the Ritual Meditation to discover your Nemeton. You went further. Your trance was deeper. But does this mean you could have gotten off at Step Five on your imagined staircase to meet your spirit guides? Possibly, but let's explore some more.

Another way to enter a trance and make contact with your Spirit Guide is called automatic writing. That means you sit down with a pad of paper and a pen and start scribbling away, writing down whatever comes to mind. For some people, this is a bit of a toughie, although others take to it right away. It's one of the methods I use quite a bit, since messages start coming to me while I'm doing something else—like making notes for this book, or mindlessly doodling.

In automatic writing, as with all spiritual contact, confidence is the key. Believe in yourself. Don't waste valuable time wondering: "Is this a spiritual message or my overactive imagination?" We are told that creative pursuits come from the soul and that is easy to believe. So, if imagination is the driving force behind creative writing and all the other fine arts, why can't it serve as the spark for your spiritual connections—the key to unlocking your soul's messages? It can and does. By blending the transition from imagining to channeling, you create a smooth and seamless bond. After a bit of practice, you'll come to trust the results and rely on the messages you receive as truth.

In my childhood, there was another option my parents used that isn't employed very much anymore—the séance. It uses outside devices to contact spirit friends, but I honestly don't recommend it for the beginner. I can and do use this technique at times, but that is after years of watching and experiencing all the workings of such a method. You see, devices like the Clan Mothers' three-legged oak divining stool, or a round table, or quasi-entertainment games like the Ouija board should carry big warning signs and lots of clear instructions for use. Why? Although such devices can and do work for almost anyone, they so often attract those lost or downtrodden souls I mentioned earlier. The lesser beings flock to amateur seances. And the devices themselves attract tricksters, too, from both sides of the earthplane. The real problem is that most devices for spirit contact are usually used by novices and by people just out looking for a thrill or, sadly, by unscrupulous individuals looking to deceive or to manipulate you. Stay well clear of this spiritual sideshow. You don't need it.

Since you have already gained deep meditative experience when you undertook the journey to your sacred Nemeton, why not build on that recent success? If you want to meet your Spirit Guide, I recommend we go back to that sacred place—your Nemeton. It's a natural and comfortable venue in which to further extend your personal magick powers. It's simple and foolproof. Don't you agree? I thought you would.

Spirit Guides help us know ourselves

Discovering and convening with a Spirit Guide was a practice common to a whole range of early cultures, especially among those many Celtic Clans that followed the Goddess.

Within the principles of the Old Way, the Clan Mothers felt that a Spirit Guide helped a young tribal woman on her way to understanding exactly who she was. This fundamental information—recognizing who you are—was one of the pillars of the Goddess faith. And this life slogan is literally carved in stone. Anthropologists and other academic researchers have found numerous stone "dolmen," structures consisting of a long stone perched like a beam on top of two tall standing stones, and many other large stones inside ancient burial mounds, engraved with lettering that relays this simple message: **To thy Self first be True.**

Your Spirit Guide will help you do just that. And since no one can ever be loved too much, welcoming your guide into your daily life will add yet another loving soul to your circle—one more presence who fully approves of you. Wow, you'd be a fool not to shout out, "Bring it on!" So let's gather up the basic Sacred Tools for your Tinder Box and travel back to your Nemeton to meet a wonderful friend.

Quick Minute Magick: Ritual Mediation To Meet Your Spirit Guide

Consult the instructions for the Quick Minute Magick in the previous chapter about finding your Nemeton. The journey is basically the same, although there are different herbs to help you on your way. Though you won't actually do the ceremony, you will imagine the spicy scents of all the herbs used in this ritual. The ritual mediation will return you to your Nemeton, but this time someone will be waiting for you. Don't get nervous. It's your best of best friends—your main Spirit Guide—who has known and loved you since you drew your first gasping breath on the earthplane.

By now you know the absolute essentials needed as you walk through the ceremony in your mind: cast the Spell of Protection, make the Power Fist, say, "Mother-Mine," and then vividly imagine all the other steps in the ritual. Read the Tinder Box of Sacred Tools carefully as if you were gathering up all the essential ingredients. The trigger to conjure up your guide is not a physical act like the Thumb of Knowledge. It is a verbal trigger—the simple act of calling your guide's name—which you will learn in your meditation.

And remember three essential bits of advice:

> One: You are always in control and may stop whenever you choose.
> Two: You have nothing to fear for you are surrounded by loving beings.
> Three: You are never alone.

Although the steps of your ritual meditation leading to your sacred place are exactly the same, I have included some special visionary bath herbs, ceremonial herbs, and a spray of Rowan (Mountain Ash) Berries and leaves, if you are able to find them. The herbs and incense have stimulating and joyful properties that wake up the senses, and are helpful for spirit contact. You will prepare the ceremonial herbs differently and use them to anoint yourself.

Silver is the metal of the Goddess. Like her moonlight, it reflects and directs the strong forces of Good and should be worn if you have any. There are also a few other specialized Sacred Tools to help and guide you toward this enlightening spirit meeting.

Tinder Box of Sacred Tools
Ritual Mediation To Meet Your Spirit Guide

Ceremonial Herbs: Crush one clove of fresh garlic. Mix with 1 tsp. of Paprika, 1 tsp. of dried Angelica, and 1 tsp. powdered Ginger. Add water to make a paste. 1 fresh apple.

Cauldron: Simmer 6 lemon slices, 6 orange slices, 1 tbs. Star Anise or dried Fennel, 1 stick of Cinnamon, or 1 tsp. powder in 2 cups of water on the stove for about 10 minutes. Let sit for a few minutes, then pour all into your warm bathtub, or use essential oils with lemon and orange slices added for the fun of it. 2 quarter-inch thick slices of fresh Cucumber for your eyes.

Witch's Brew: Peppermint tea with 1 tsp. of Mugwort and a slice of lemon.

Incense: Either Peppermint, Lavender, or some with strong spicy scent.

Tree Amulet: A spray of Mountain Ash leaves with berries.

Elements: Your choice, but try to include a white candle that has been daubed with your own perfume. For Earth use metal, silver bracelets, rings, or necklaces to reflect the light.

Flagon: Spiced Rum in Orange juice, or Cranberry with sparkling water or any spicy or effervescent libation.

Celtic Bard: Your absolute favorite music. Play softly throughout the ceremony.

Storyteller: Before the ceremony, try to watch the film, *The Secrets of Ronan Innish*. The spirit protectors are seals or Silkies as some of the coastal Celts called them.

Discovery: Place a pen and paper close to your chair to record your experience.

Clan of the Goddess

The significance of these Sacred Tools and how to use them

Cauldron: The fruity/spicy mixture that you simmer on the stove and add to your bath is designed to wake up your spirit. To stimulate your senses. Anise (try to get the star-shaped variety because it's pretty and fun to watch floating in your bath) is an herb that aids in seeking answers from the Otherworld (Fennel is a suitable substitute). Cinnamon is excellent for opening the portals between the planes to allow for ease of internal communication. It is also an excellent help in meditating.

Cucumber is known as a natural beauty aid to soothe the delicate tissues around the eyes. It does the same spiritually, opening your spiritual eye which is also called the third eye. You can't see it, but it is located in the middle of your forehead between your eyebrows and just above your nose. When people are really stressed, they often squeeze or rub this area, because their soul doesn't like what it's seeing. The third eye is considered the center of positive intuition, encouraging you to both "See and Know."

Incense: The incense, as always, is lit in your bathroom, then moved to your living room. For this ritual the incense should have a Peppermint or Spearmint scent, since Mint increases your ability to see into the Otherworld. Lavender, if you chose that instead, is another strong visionary herb that helps usher in all that is good and loving.

Ceremonial Herbs: The method of anointing yourself in this ritual is different from the times you threw a dry herb mixture in the air like confetti. This time, make a wet paste of crushed Garlic, Sweet Paprika (be sure you don't mistake it for red Cayenne—it will burn) plus a teaspoon of dried Angelica and another of powdered Ginger. Add a pinch of sugar and mix it all briskly with confident determination for you are a Celtic Diviner, stirring up your natural spiritual remedy. Add water a few drops at a time until the consistency is like soft peanut butter. Smell it. Breathe in all its natural properties and think of the Clan Mothers choosing and mixing this exact formula to aid their spiritual journey. You should make this in advance and place it near your chair in the living room.

Why did you combine these particular herbs? Garlic, an ancient protection against the dreaded "evil eye" of early superstitions, will banish any unwanted forces or silly tricksters with great efficiency so you'll have no worries of being disturbed. Paprika and Ginger are stimulating herbs to refresh and enliven your inner senses, and invigorate your soul. Angelica was a favorite herb of early Celtic midwives because it was a reliable aid for both mother and child in the life-changing journey of birth. It will protect and aid you on your journey to other realities, and allow you to enjoy thoroughly the sacred time "betwixt and between" in your meditation.

Apples were sacred to the Celtic Clan Mothers because they are so strong in attracting the light and amplifying the effects of the Forces of Good. Avalon, the Celtic version of heaven, actually translates as "Appleland." When cut right across its middle, the Apple reveals the clear shape of the pentagram, another ancient symbol. The presence of the Apple pleases the spirits and the faeries. Your uncut Apple is an ancient symbol of respect for, and an offering to, those loving spirits in the Otherworld.

Tree Amulet: Your spray of leaves, twigs, and Rowan berries (Mountain Ash) has a long history of protection, good health and good fortune. I'm fortunate to have two Rowan trees in my backyard. I can see the larger one as I sit here writing to you. I have two more trees standing sentinel in the front. Watching them change over the seasons is a delight. It is easy to see why they were so treasured by the ancients, and why so many spiritual qualities were assigned to them. In spring, they are covered with small, white and lacy bouquets of star-shaped blossoms. In summer, their green berries slowly turn a burnt orange, and their cooling shade is dense and inviting. In fall, the berries deepen to blood red. By late fall, huge flocks of beautiful Cedar Waxwings with black bandit masks arrive to fuel up on the vitamin-rich berries for their long journey south. Literally hundreds chomp away, sometimes hanging upside down like circus acrobats to the delight of all who see them.

In the winter, the remaining red Rowan berry clusters catch and hold white cones of snow until the big tree appears covered in upside down ice cream cones. By the following spring, there are still enough dried berries left to welcome back the early returning and ravenous Waxwings, who dine there once again while the gusty spring storms blow through. The Rowan tree's presence at your ceremony assures peace of mind and a calm heart.

The Celts always planted a Mountain Ash tree close to their homes. It kept unwanted forces at bay and provided a dome of Goddess protection over all who dwelled near. Rowan is a powerful charm and when more focus was needed on the positive aspects of spirituality, sprays of leaves and berries were cut and brought inside, or its wood was hung outside over the doorway to the cottage. Mothers would often sew a sprig of Rowan into their children's garments to ward off any untoward influences for those times when the little ones were away from their mother's watchful eye. Its scarlet berries were considered food for the Goddess and that is why it was so highly esteemed.

When you sit down to meditate during the ceremony, pick up the Rowan branch and hold it in your right hand. You may even brush it over your hair and your shoulders, and lightly touch it to your heart. **Beware: don't put the berries to your lips for they are poisonous to humans.**

Witch's Brew: For the same purpose of stimulation, you will brew a cup of Peppermint tea with an added teaspoon of Mugwort with Lemon (and some honey if you wish). Sip it as you listen to your favorite music just before you begin your ritual. And don't forget the benefits of inhaling herbal steam water from the spiraling vapors just above the rim of your mug.

The Elements: As with all representations of the sacred elements at your rituals, place them near your chair but not in the way when you stand. Earth may be represented by salt, a rock, a plate of real soil, or any small vessel made from clay. For the representation of Air, you can use a feather, a corked bottle of air, a lovely fan, or any other clear representation of breezes or flight. Water can simply be a glass or pitcher of pure water, a seashell, or some memorabilia that once lived in or near a lake or ocean. For the Element of Fire, you will be using a white candle that has been rubbed earlier with a bit of your own perfume to help draw your Spirit Guide to you. Remember to blow lightly on the candle and watch the flame bow softly away, and then return. The air in your lungs is the sweet, life-giving breath of your Goddess within. Take a moment to recall your sacred divinity, because you really are beginning to believe it now, aren't you?

Flagon: The completion of this ceremony will be worth celebrating because you will be aware of a welcome, but unseen, guest attending your party. The spicy alcoholic or non-alcoholic drink will remind you of all that your are: sparkling, zesty, and chock-full of shimmering life.

Metal: Silver is the choice for tonight as it draws down the power of the Mother Moon and reflects the light of the candle, just as your life reflects the sacredness within you. Be sure it is well-polished and wear it all the time if you like. The Goddess loves you in silver.

Celtic Storyteller: Although watching the video, *The Secret of Ronan Innish,* isn't a necessity, it does get you in the mood for appreciating the Celtic Ancestors and their gentle, nurturing way of teaching youngsters. In this film it is a Grandmother and Grandfather who take in their granddaughter. Through their protection and love, and some supernatural helpers, the girl finds her long-lost brother. It illustrates the importance of believing beyond that which is normally seen to be true. It's a happy story and it is food for the soul.

Discovery: The pad of writing paper is for you to record, as soon as the ritual is finished, the information you received through your guide: their name as you understood it, their message and anything else about them you don't want to forget. The issue of Spirit Guide names is worth mentioning here, because spirit names are often archaic, odd-sounding or simply names made up for humans to use as a trigger to call on them. I've had my guides tell me that names are of no consequence whatsoever, that calling for "My Spirit Guide" would be sufficient. However, once a name is offered or agreed upon and established, it is an easy way to summon your guide. It also makes everything more personal, and that could mean more powerful, too.

This is important to remember: whatever name first comes to you, accept it, no matter how strange or how simple it is. Don't question it. It will pop into your mind and that name will be the key to contacting your Spirit Guide. They may also tell you a bit about themselves: when they walked the face of Abred; what their profession or occupation was; or you may simply guess this by their dress.

Spiritual insurance: A simple way to banish unwanted visitors

Now, there is a very small possibility you will not feel comfortable when a spirit approaches. You may feel that the one presented to you is a bit of a trickster, that it feels heavy or burdened in some way, or just "not right." Trust your keen woman's instincts. If that unlikely scenario occurs, you can simply banish that unwanted presence instantly. Tell them to go away and they will. And remember, if you feel the need, you can open your eyes for a moment to remind yourself how safe you are in your home and that you are in total control.

When you feel your confidence return, close you eyes and go back to your Nemeton. Ask again for your higher Spirit Guide to attend you. If you are still uncomfortable, simply end the ritual right there and try another day. No worries.

Summary of steps to meeting your Spirit Guide

Let's review the steps and where everything goes in preparation for the ritual in the bath:

- ❖ a candle and incense set up in the bathroom.
- ❖ your ceremonial costume hanging on the back of the door.
- ❖ silver bangles and jewelry ready to be slipped on.
- ❖ a pot of simmered herbs, spices, and fruit from the kitchen added to your bath water.
- ❖ two freshly cut cucumber slices waiting by the tub.

In your kitchen: the Witch's Brew:

- ❖ Peppermint tea with Mugwort and Lemon waiting for the boiling water.

In the living room:

❖ the Elements are set around your chair.

❖ your herbal visionary paste is beside it.

❖ a branch of Rowan leaves and berries on the arm of the chair.

❖ a white candle, already scented with your favorite perfume.

❖ your very favorite music playing softly, yet loudly enough to pick up a hint in the bathroom.

I do believe, lovely lady, that you are set.

Light your incense and bathroom candle, pour the spicy simmered mixture into the full tub, climb in and lean back. Place one cucumber slice on each of your closed eyelids. While you relax, sing or hum along to the music drifting in from the living room. Imagine all your fears, all your worries, all your stress is flowing out the tips of your fingers and your 10 little toes. Wiggle them and shake your finger tips free of all your cares. Breathe in the fragrance of the bath water and the smoky incense. Go ahead and giggle if an orange slice, a star Anise, or Cinnamon stick bumps into your naked arms or knees while your eyes are shielded by the cucumbers. Try poking at the floaters with your fingers, or swirl the water and feel them race by you in the whirlpool.

Now heed me here! If any worrisome thoughts come sneaking into your head, say out loud, "No, not you! Go away. You are not wanted on this voyage." Then consciously recall one of the happy memories you have stored in your Power Fist, one of those fabulous moments when you were blissful and felt the presence of the joy of the Goddess. This is your time to wallow in joyful memories of happy times. Squeeze your Power Fist, say, "Mother-Mine," and feel the divine energy surge up your left arm and through your body. All is well.

On to the Ritual Mediation

When you feel the purification bath is complete, remove the cucumbers slices from your eyes, then, before you emerge, cast your Spell of Protection around your whole body. See the shimmering radiance of that misty light envelope you in everlasting protection. Step out of the tub and fish out the large floating pieces of fruit or herbs, using your fingers as a net. Pull the plug and wave good-bye to all your worries, all the tension you released. Towel off with enthusiasm while you hum along with your favorite songs. Slip on your costume, along with the silver jewelry. Make it jingle. Catch the dancing reflection of the candle's flame on your silver rings, brooches, or bangles. Imagine the Great Mother's dancing moonlight reflected there. Blow out the candle and carry the incense to your living room.

Whip up your cup of Witch's Brew and sip it as you sit in your chair and breathe deeply of the steam water spiraling up from the top of the mug. If your musical choice is a sprightly tune, get up and dance about barefoot if it moves you. When you feel ready, start your meditation ritual.

Place your perfumed candle safely on the floor, or a small table to the north. Light it and enjoy its spirited movements as you blow softly on it. Follow the same initial steps you did in the Nemeton ritual mediation: make your Power Fist and say, "Mother-Mine." feel the energy of the Goddess move through you and thank Her for Her attendance; welcome the energy of the Airts, the four compass points; cast your Golden Circle big enough to include your chair; then sit back down.

Put your right index finger in the paste and rub a small amount on your third eye—between your eyes and slightly above your eyebrows. Picture this energy chakra opening as a small, whirling cone of indigo light at the exact place you have anointed it. Feel it tingle as your energy opens. Say, "Great

Mother, with this herbal paste I anoint my third eye. Help open my inner vision to see and know my Spirit Guide—a visitor from the Otherworld, a loving gift from You to me."

Pick up your Rowan spray. Brush your hair, your arms, your heart and your legs gently with the branch. Hold it in your right hand (your left is still in a comfortable Power Fist). Begin the exact steps from your Nemeton mediation ritual. That is: relax with three deep breaths; imagine yourself standing in front of you watching yourself as you sit in the chair; then turn and, while you look at your bare feet, move toward the staircase where you will first see your Oaken Door. You know it now. You recognize it. It is a beautiful masterpiece; a work of art as are you. Rap three times with confidence, open it inward and pass through to find yourself at the top of the stairs. Watch your feet carefully while you see and feel each step. Count slowly from one to 10, giving each step a number and telling yourself that you are going deeper with each step. At the last step, you see your Nemeton before you, your very own sacred place just as it was last time. You love the feeling of being there. Enter and walk about, then sit quietly down. Relax.

Now turn to your left and look down a long narrow road. It can be any kind of path or road that fits with your Nemeton: sandy, rocky, or hardened dirt. Someone is walking toward you and you are glad to see that person because you know each other. This is a glorious reunion.

When that person stands before you, say with heartfelt feeling, "Welcome friend of mine." Your guide becomes clear to you now and comfortably familiar. You may find yourself smiling. He or she greets you. How does he do that? It may be shyly, or with a strong voice full of confidence, or with a relaxed sense of mirth, or perhaps the greeting is a simple nod. Without asking, he will declare himself. Spirit Guides always do. With your mind, not your ears, you will hear your Spirit Guide's voice in your head as he announces to you, "I am . . ."

Trust what you hear. You aren't making it up. Repeat the name so you won't forget it. You will probably get it the first time. But, if it's particularly difficult to remember, ask your Guide to spell it out or repeat it, until you can say it—or some form of it. This is important to establish for it is the trigger to call forth your Spirit Guide whenever you wish. If the name still isn't clear, ask if you can use something like Special Friend, or another name. You will soon come to some agreement on a name that will please you both.

Your Spirit Guide may tell you about herself or talk about the task of guiding you. She may even remind you of a time when you called for help from above and she came to your aid. You will find the conversation passing easily back and forth in your mind. Feel free to ask questions like: "How long have you been my guide?" or "Will you come to me when I call you?" If your Spirit Guide is willing, you may ask about her life on Earth, if she traveled here, what she did, who she was, what country she lived in, and when. Many Spirit Guides are very old souls and, for whatever reason, their time on Earth may no longer be significant; in which case, they may tell you about their work in the Otherworld, as my Uncle Joe did when he mentioned his work with injured animals.

If she had an earthly identity, ask about the place where she lived, although if it was eons ago, that place may not be readily recognizable today. When she describes her span of time on the earthplane, it may sound as if she is speaking in metaphors or a quoting from a lovely poem. In fact, you'll probably find her speech is very elegant, even flowery. That is common. The important thing is that you are getting to know each other and you may be pleasantly surprised to find some things you have in common that may have relevance to your own interests, profession, or creative pursuits. She may have lived in a certain country that has always intrigued you, or where you once traveled.

If you have a particularly pressing problem, tell your guide and ask for his advice. He may not have a ready-made solution, because much of his work is to help you find your own way out of situations, to literally 'guide you.' But you will either get some insight, or renewed confidence that he will be supporting your efforts to solve your problem in the future.

Your first visit may be short. Thank your Spirit Guide by the name you learned, or both agreed upon, then take your leave. That is easy to do because he is not left behind in your Nemeton. He is always close by you. Like the Goddess, and like your soul, he is a part of the bigger you.

Proceed to the stairs, go back up counting down from 10 to one, go through the door, and return to your comfortable chair. Open your eyes and notice how great you feel. You feel light and excited and happy, all at the same time. But you aren't finished yet. Stand up and bid your farewell to the energies of the Airts, thank the Goddess for Her gift to you this day, and close the circle counter-clockwise with formality and respect. You're done. Isn't it amazing? You are no longer a solo traveler on this life journey. What's more, you are well aware of it.

You may have this strong urge to call me up on the telephone and say, *"C.C. you were right. I met my Spirit Guide and now I know in my heart that I am never alone."* I don't have a phone number that's accessible, but you can share your experience by visiting my Web site, listed at the end of the book. I'd be thrilled to share this joy with you. Oh, and if you weren't able to fully identify your guide, I'll be glad to assist you through the Internet connection.

One more thing before you carry out your Celtic celebration. You must take a moment to write a few scraps of information down about your guide. His or her name, any message, or any other bit you don't want to forget. Don't get formal, you can fill out the details later.

Now the celebration. *Yahoo*! The spicy drink. The wild Celt in you jumping about, laughing like some kind of half-crazed hyena. Turn up the music. Talk to your Spirit Guide. Thank her again—she can hear you and I would bet my bottom dollar she is smiling too, and radiating with the joy of this soul connection. You just made her job a whole lot easier!

Well, my divine Goddess, how do you feel now? Pretty spectacular, I bet, and so you should. You're getting very accomplished in the spiritual arts and in mastering the women's mysteries. And you can begin to see how the teachings and magical techniques of those wonderful Clan Mothers of yesteryear helped women make it through the roughest of times, can't you? History may call these teachings part of the Old Way, but it was good for women. It was a faith that stressed the importance of elder wisewomen fully preparing their daughters for life's journey. Having your Spirit Guide as a loving and wise friend beside you is part of that preparation. Blessed be.

Now that you know your Spirit Guide, what happens in your relationship from now on?

How to communicate with your Spirit Guide

The legends and literature of the early Celts is full of examples of the easy and relaxed relationship enjoyed between humans and supernatural beings. They believed that the more developed among them—Diviners, wisewomen, and many of the elders, most of whom were women—lived comfortably with "one foot on either side of the river." In other words, straddling the two realities of the earthplane and the Otherworld. And when it came to everyday stories of shapeshifting, of dancing the night away with faeries or of visitations from spirits, no one blinked an eye. It was all part of their daily experience, their culture. Having a Spirit Guide that you chatted with was as commonplace and familiar as having a good friend next door. And so it should be. It is a natural state of operating. And maybe much of today's fundamental stress is related to losing that innate human/spirit bond. Spirit helpers have always been there. Now let's tap into that remarkable resource. Here's how you communicate when you talk with your Spirit Guide. First, as with all your magick, cast the instant Spell of Protection around yourself; squeeze your left fist into a Power Fist; whisper, "Mother-Mine," and ask your guide, by name, to come to you.

Mission accomplished. In less than 10 seconds, you have all the spiritual help you will ever need. Just relax, open up, and pay attention to the thoughts that come to mind. And if you have relied on ancestors or guardian angels in the past, call for them at the same time—the more help and guidance the better. But don't make it complicated, difficult, or full of angst. It's simple and effortless. You simply hear your Spirit Guide in your thoughts. Be a self-assured Goddess. This is what strong intuition is all about, isn't it? Or hunches. They are strong, clear messages from the soul.

If, by chance, you are unsure of the connection with your Spirit Guide—if it isn't as clear as your first meeting—go no further. Instead, return to your Nemeton in a formal ritual mediation trance and ask to meet there a few more times, until it all becomes so familiar, so second nature, that you can do it effortlessly in your waking state as well.

You'll know in your heart of hearts, when your Spirit Guide is sending you a message. It will be something quite different from your usual train of thought and you'll soon learn to recognize it, because the message is seldom what you would normally expect. Something so off the wall, you never would have made it up. Take this example: You're having trouble with someone at work who is a spiteful, damaging gossip. You are so tense working with that person, it is making you sick from stress. You dread getting up out of bed and going to work. Her darkness is coloring everything in your life and all for the worse. Got the situation? You've experienced such, I'm sure.

So, go to your Spirit Guide for direction. In the serenity of your home that night, cast your magick and call the name of your guide. Be assured, your Spirit Guide is there instantly. Then you simply ask: "What should I do about this terrible, spiteful person at work? I'm being driven to distraction." You'll hear the answer as your own thoughts. Trust this. You may think you are only "making up" the answer—but wait—it may be a surprising answer, one that never crossed your mind, or wouldn't in a million years. The voice in your head says something like this: "Change you tactics. This person is a lonely, hurting soul. Bring this troublemaker flowers tomorrow. Just smile and gift her." Yikes! That's the last thing you would have thought, because you are a long way past compassion for this vile person. So, what the heck, you try it. The nasty one is flabbergasted. The advice was good, because you can see you've disarmed the troublemaker, neutralized your problem with kindness.

That's how easily it happens. It's so simple, yet it is hard to fathom. But I promise, after two or three positive experiences you will truly believe the good advice you thought you were only imagining. Practice is the key. Soon, you'll fine tune the relationship, develop your own methods of following guidance and hearing positive and encouraging spiritual advice from the knowing side, from the Otherworld. And it will always be with the blessed goal of making your life more meaningful, richer and more fulfilling.

Here's another tip about heavenly helpers. They are delighted to be called upon. Don't be shy. It doesn't have to be an earth-shaking situation. Going into a tough meeting? Simply ask for help and guidance to say the right thing. Feeling shaky before getting up to speak in front of people? Ask your

Guide to be there with you, to stop the jitters and make you shine in front of that audience. Trouble with your teenager? Ask for help in finding the wise and understanding words to say to get the best response. Hoping to deepen the passion in your love life? Just ask the guides to help you enhance the charms of the feminine divine within. Go ahead. Ask for help in intimate situations. You are astonished? No need to be. Remember, those wild and lusty Celts believed firmly that lovemaking was a direct gift from the Goddess to all Her children. Like everything else in your life now, enjoy to the optimum all the many pleasures of Abred.

I could list a million reasons for calling on your Spirit Guide, but the best one is to get in the everyday habit of reaching out to receive your wisest, most loving counsel. Soon you'll find that you are widening your understanding of people and their deepest motivations and, in so doing, you'll come to truly know yourself. So there you have it.

Congratulations! You skilled and cunning Goddess you. You've met the truest friend you'll ever have. You are on the path to becoming the best you ever can be.

Part 2:

Using Your Woman's Magick to Enrich Your Life

Using Your Woman's Magick

Chapter Six

Victory Over Past Sorrows and Haunting Shadows

You've mastered your personal power and magick. You've found that sacred place, your Nemeton, and you walk tall and proud beside your Spirit Guide. With the renewed confidence the Goddess has given you, it's now time to address the darker side of your past, of your nature; to acknowledge and take control of the shadowland of your life. We'll do it successfully, using a magick stew of ancient legends and lessons, Clan Mother wisdom that echoes elements of modern psychotherapy.

The Celtic Mother Goddess, the nurturer, also had a dark and somber side. She taught that the cycles of light and darkness, happiness and sorrow, life and death always go hand-in-hand. One cannot be present without the other fast behind to balance life. It's a hard concept to accept in the "feel-good" environment of the Western world, but recognizing the need for this delicate balance during stressful times will give you strength as you wait for positive events to return to your life, as they surely do.

Using a number of protective and calming herbal formulas, along with a dip in your bathtub, the Great Mother's Cauldron of Regeneration and Rebirth, you will be ready to take part in a ritual to take the best and discard the negative. How? You'll learn to give credence to what you've learned from your hard times and the value it gave to some aspect of who you are today. In the same ritual, you will also learn to eliminate or diminish the negative impact of the dark side of your mind. The goal being one of balance and control.

For this Banishing Ritual, you'll use a three-pronged approach to quieting the inner demons: a potion of the ancient **Celtic Draught of Forgetfulness**; the ritual casting of the **Spell to Banish Fear**; and a life-altering session in your steaming Cauldron bath where you'll employ the ancient arts of **Shapeshifting with Invisibility** to slip away from your shadows. These time-honored approaches to soul work will include an added dash of **visualization** techniques to spice up the whole adventure. You'll emerge lighter of heart and mind, with a new strength of conviction. You'll be clearer about what you don't want in your life; and you'll have a firm hold on the reins of those monsters that used to haunt you. They'll become your humble servants, instead of your persecutors. Past sorrows and bad experiences will no longer cause anxiety attacks, or trip you up with unexpected bouts of depression.

The Goddess will show you how to disconnect the constant barrage of negative memories and recriminations that sap your energy and pull you down. The dark side will meekly submit to your authority, to be used in the future only to your advantage, as one of your inner helpers. Along with this psychic release of memories that are shrouded with darkness and pain, light will pour into that opened up space, and you'll have much more room for the joy that you so deserve. Who can beat that? Ready for the great house cleaning that just might save your life?

Goddess wisdom regarding the shadows in your life

The Clan Mothers believed that the gift of an abundant and prosperous life was earned. They taught women to accept that we are all here to travel the rocky road, to hold on tight through the hairpin turns, and to develop keen navigating skills as a result. They knew that without experiencing life's challenges and overcoming its sorrows, those gifts of abundance—those sparkly little packages of bounty—were of little value and largely without meaning. The price of a good life was to triumph over adversity.

They knew, as you do in your own heart, that only by knowing sorrow, heartache, or even poor health firsthand, are we able to feel genuine compassion for others and to have empathy for other women—our dear sisters. To the Clan Mothers, the courage to meet your hardships head on and have the staying power to live to tell about it, were admirable traits that counted as a measure of your soul's depth. They were part of your kit bag of earthly riches. Let's face it, those old women were scrappers, and they would urge you to be one, too. The Goddess is tough. She is gentle and kind, but firm. She'd want you to climb into the ring and stand strong and fight the good fight. They considered survivors, like you, to be the truly blessed ones.

I know, I can hear you grumbling. If life is supposed to be so hard, you want off this Celtic merry-go-round right now. But wait. Life isn't all hardships and trials. Yes, they taught us that we must accept suffering and change as part of the human condition, but they also told us that we were free to make choices—free, in effect, to design the components of our life. And that's not so bad.

I can't help but be reminded of the so-called Chinese curse, "May you live in interesting times." The Clan Mothers would have considered this a fair and proper blessing. Certainly it carries the ominous portents of tragedy, change, and loss; but it also offers equal possibilities for wonder, growth, and enlightenment. Remember, suffering and enduring make it possible for you to stretch and grow spiritually, to develop an insightful appreciation for all the good and yummy things in life. Now, if you don't like the sound of that, don't blame me: the Clan Mothers deserve your rebuke. They taught us to embrace the dark side of life's journey and view it as an opportunity to rise above—to show what stuff we are truly made of. They were spiritual, but they were pragmatists.

The truth is you have already suffered, dear friend, haven't you? We all have in different ways and to different degrees—some horrifically. What you really need is help in sorting it all out, in understanding it and developing some wisdom relating to those dreadful experiences. As a first step, we'll get rid of the legacy of some of those past hurts that still manage to haunt you. There are three conscious changes for you to make in order to put these hard experiences aside, while wringing every last bit of goodness from them before they take a hike. They are:

> Change your attitude.
> Give those memories the credit they deserve.
> Learn to remember to forget.

Easy as pie. Here's how to do it.

1. **Change your attitude.** That's right. Come to your problems of yesteryear with a completely fresh outlook. Stand in your today shoes in order to view those sorrows. Don't stand in your baby booties or your teen-aged sneakers, or even last year's high heels. You've changed. You've grown. Look on them from the vantage point of all you have learned and experienced. By updating your attitude to the here and now, you'll diminish the

influence of those old memories and put them in their place—a place of much less importance. Pledge to toughen up and move those disruptive bullies to the back seat in your classroom. No more center stage, that's reserved for your joys—for more love, laughter, and happiness. Yes! Good first step. Blessed be.

2. **Give those bad memories the credit they deserve.** Yikes! Isn't that a contradiction? Didn't we just shoo them away with their tails between their legs? Indeed, and you were good at it. But what I'm saying about the value of your dark shadows is still part of the tough-girl attitude, it's just a little bit complicated, like one of those intricate Celtic knots. I'll try to explain. Almost every bad experience or painful heartache you have suffered has taught you something. Come on, admit it. Now, a few of your sorrows may seem to have little or no merit. Why so? Is it because the benefit from that particular experience might be on a much deeper soul level, and not readily apparent at the moment? Think about it. But most of your other bad experiences ultimately served as life lessons, didn't they?

The wisdom of the Clan Mothers often sprang from analyzing their own litany of bitter and/or foolish experiences. In turn, they offer this undeniable truth—every mistake you've made, bad bargain you've agreed to, questionable lover you should have slammed the door on but didn't, foolish indulgence that turned sour, pain inflicted on you from outside your will, and every trip of your quick tongue that hurt others and ultimately yourself (need I go on?), were all teaching tools. Tools designed specifically to help your soul learn and grow. Make no mistake, these custom-tailored lessons belong to no one else but you. To boil it down to the basics: the more mistakes you make; the more opportunities you have to learn.

You've certainly learned what "not" to do, right? Life's knocks have made you cautious and taught you signals to look for in the future. You are a warrior with keen senses, not the victim, the hunted, the prey. In large measure, you were fashioned and sculpted by the trials you survived. You were reinvented as a wiser soul. You grew in some way, that's for sure, and most likely you are hardened by the experiences but—listen to me—hard is good. It is. Hard does not have to be brittle. Hard is forged strength. Hard means you can never be hurt in that very same way, ever again. Hard knocks give you the materials to fashion yourself a Lorica—a breastplate of protection—hammered together from the pieces of your heart and soul that were shattered and broken. Nothing was lost. You turned bad into good. You are a mystical alchemist, a modern-day miracle maker. A magician.

But still, the question begs: if you got some measure of value from your past sorrows and dark shadows, why do they haunt you still? Why does your mind reenact the sadness over and over? It's a fair question. Let's just say these instant replays, these endless tape loops, have long overstayed their welcome. They're using up the tiny bit of good they delivered. It's time to cut your losses.

3. **Learn to remember to forget.** What kind of cock-eyed Celtic fireside riddle is that? Well, it means just what it says. There is a time to let go and to consciously remind yourself to forget. Clear as mud? It means you need to train your mind to forget the details of your troubles, and to forget the raw pain you still feel. And especially to forget any humiliation or feelings of worthlessness. You need a strategy to run those negative memories out of your everyday life. It's time to fold

them up, smooth them down, and lock them away. Toss the key over your left shoulder and keep on walking. Face it, those old hurts have outlived their usefulness, but they have this cocky swagger like they've got a life of their own, muscling into your thoughts and shoving all the good stuff out of the way. They are an unwanted energy that's been allowed to grow and flourish, because you didn't have the means to disarm them—the witch's magick broom to sweep them out the door, once and for all. Now you will.

And after you learn to forget, I will lead you in a ritual to banish the pain in your past, to become the producer, director, and leading lady of all the movies that play and replay exclusively at the theater in your mind. It is a creative adventure steeped in Celtic wisdom and tradition that has proven results. And there is a double benefit in store: banishing those awful memories from a prime role in your life leaves a vacuum to be filled with all the brightness and joy you can imagine. Consciously agree with me to forget, and the healing begins. Believe it.

The ancient legends of the Draught of Forgetfulness

The Clan Mothers gained their understanding of the value of purposely forgetting from an ancient Celtic legend, which was told and retold by the bards around crackling bonfires and warm central hearths in cottages across ancient Britain. This legend is about inner pain and suffering so terrible that, in order to survive, the emotional burden had to be laid down and a spell cast to forget. It's a sort of template for what you must do to let go of your own pain, or the heartbreak you've suffered to the point of obsession. This is how the legend goes:

Cuchullin was a famous Celtic hero who fell madly, hopelessly in love with the beautiful goddess Fand, the wife of the sea god Mananna. When her husband reclaimed her, and took her away to his watery empire under the ocean, Cuchullin was wild with anguish and sorrow. Try as he would, he grieved so deeply for his lost love that in the throes of his obsession he wanted only to die. The wise Druids formulated the Draught of Forgetfulness so that he would forget Fand and begin to remember to live again. He drank a potion from their cupped hands and her memory troubled his heart and soul no more. He was freed from the hopeless infatuation that threatened his very survival. He learned the art of remembering to forget.

What is noteworthy is that the Clan Mothers and the Druidic sages linked the acts of healing with forgetting. And they were right. Often, before healing of the heart, the mind and, in some case, the body can take place, the process of forgetting has to happen.

We will access the very power and healing energy found in the Celtic tradition of the Draught of Forgetfulness. In our banishing ritual, we will symbolically tap into this ancient power to make you "sound from every sickness."

Ancient tricks to help women disassociate from internal demons

The Wisewomen of the Clan of the Goddess were so connected to nature, and the powers and sensitivity of its spirits, that they would often send troubled women out to lie among the grasses and wildflowers to help heal themselves. My own mother once sent me out on a lovely summer day to lie on my back in a meadow, to help ease a terrible memory that I couldn't seem to shake. It was several years after the fact when I confessed to her that it still had power over me in the quiet times, or in the middle of the night. She immediately packed me off to the Great Mother's loving arms—just me and nature and its numinous healing properties. Mother's instructions that day were the lessons she herself had learned as a girl.

She said to lie in the grasses and bring forward the very worst part my bad memory, the painful part, until it was foremost in my mind. I was to do this with as little emotional involvement as possible. This, of course, was difficult because I had memorized each awful detail—we women can get very involved in our bad memories, can't we? The trick, however, was not to get involved, and after a few errant tears, I succeeded. Here is how it worked. She called it her "little woman's trick."

Big, white fluffy clouds—cumulus clouds—were moving swiftly overhead. My mother said to take the bad memory from my mind and place it up on the edge of a cloud. Picture it there, instead of inside my head and heart. I did. Then she said make that bit of cloud your hurtful memory. That terrible memory is now sailing aloft on that fast-moving cloud. Watch the cloud intently. Watch as it drifts off, changes shape, and slowly breaks up. Watch what little is left, the last feathery bit, move away across the blue sky into oblivion. See it go and believe. Your small corner of darkness is riding that spirit cloud. Leaving you forever. Carried by the breath of the Goddess. As it floats out of sight, feel it leaving you, feel the healing happening inside you. The lightness of being. It is Her gift to you. She doesn't want you to suffer any more. You've learned all you can from that unfortunate episode in your life. It is time to clean the slate and move on. Believe it and it will happen.

And if, by chance, it comes creeping back, hidden in the long shadows of a sleepless night: picture your cloud again, and it will recede and disappear. In doing this, you join the ranks of centuries upon centuries of women who have learned to cast their sorrows away, to put their overpowering problems in the arms of the Great Mother so they may be healed. It is a "little woman's trick" you can use and teach to your daughters, nieces, granddaughters or any young women in your life.

I would like to share another effective bit of natural magick that I learned from my dear friend, Elizabeth, who is a member of the Dene Tha' First Nation in northern Alberta, Canada. She is a truly generous and beautiful soul, who once shared this Elders' wisdom with me when I really needed it.

Elizabeth knew I was sorrowful, and told me about one of the Cree Elders' methods of removing the burdensome weight of sadness and troubles. She told me to watch the skies for an Eagle, and when I spotted one, to throw some tobacco into the air as an offering. Then I was to place my troubles on the Eagle's broad back. I should imagine doing so, then ask the Eagle to carry them up to the Great Spirit and ask the Grandmothers, the ancestors, for their blessing. "That will surely relieve your heavy heart," she reassured me.

It was only a few days later that an Eagle swooped down over an open pasture just beyond my porch, and I ran for the loose tobacco I had waiting. I did as she had instructed with great and solemn reverence. Then, I stood silently and watched as the Eagle circled higher and higher, spiraling in wide loops, up into the clouds until it was just a tiny speck against the pale blue sky. Then the speck disappeared. The Eagle was gone. My stubborn worries were gone too. I thanked the Great Spirit and the Grandmothers with all my heart. Thanks be to Elizabeth, for her love.

Both these women's folk methods of emotional healing are an act of disassociation. Our Banishing Ritual will teach you an updated method based on these Celtic and First Nations principles. You will be surprised how quickly joy finds you, when you make fresh room in your soul.

Start with baby steps: A cautionary warning

Before we begin, I must erect some blinking yellow lights to get your attention.

Dear friend, I can't possibly know what you have suffered in your life, what tremendous misfortunes may have befallen you on your road through Abred. It is just a fact: some women have suffered terribly—beyond comprehension. If you are among them, you have my heartfelt sympathy and compassion. Since we have been working together, you have embraced the power of the Goddess within you; you have learned the value of ritual; you have strengthened your soul, and experienced the positive effects of your own magick. It is just the beginning. As you practice, these skills will become a natural part of your everyday life and thinking. You will you grow even stronger and more sure of yourself.

If you do carry unimaginable sorrows, I recommend that you first walk through the steps of the Banishing Ritual without confronting those shadows along the way. This is a ritual to examine your past hurts and to begin to heal yourself; but if you have memories too painful to relive, I ask that you don't work on them yet. Start with baby steps until you are sure on your cosmic feet and won't stumble. Take a minor hurt in your past and deal with it first. Wait for your skills to mature before you pry the lid off any truly devastating memories from your past. **If you have such frightful shadows, then know that I am speaking directly to you—leave them alone until you have practiced this ritual and mastered it.** Even when you feel strong enough to tackle them, have a good friend present with you to walk through the process. Take advantage of the supportive qualities of sincere Sisterhood, for therein lies one of our great women's secrets of deep and effective healing.

To begin, let's get rid of the flotsam and jetsam that clogs the life-giving arteries to our soul. Together, we'll banish those blackguards from our lives—we'll send the joy thieves packing.

Preparations for the Banishing Ritual
Central Importance of the Cauldron to the Celts and to you

The symbolic importance of the Cauldron to Celtic mythology cannot be underestimated. In a sense, it served a similar purpose to the soup pots we still set simmering on our stovetops in order to nourish our loved ones. In effect, we are continuing the tradition of inviting the Great Mother to our fire altar—our kitchen stove. It's also significant that the Cauldron is never static. It is always being dipped into, refilled, boiled, and stirred. The contents float on top or are blended together, their fragrant aromas filling the entire house with "the healing fumes of the Goddess herbals," in the words of the Clan Mothers. And it's no mere coincidence that the pregnant-looking pots of old resembled the cosmic womb of the Great Mother, who birthed us and all living creatures. It is a divine gift she passed on—the ability to birth children; to birth solutions to problems; to birth new and exciting ideas; and to birth the creative forces of the soul through our art.

In early Celtic homes, the three-legged iron Cauldron, set over embers, was never empty. Its contents included all types of vegetables in season, dried beans and peas in winter, chopped bits of meat from the latest hunt, cereals and, always, a sampling of herbs and spices. The taste was never the same twice. And because the Cauldron was always simmering on the hearth, it was a given that no one ever went hungry, no one did without. A healthy portion, poured from an elaborately carved wooden ladle, would nourish the body and rejuvenate the soul. The steaming Cauldron represented bounty and abundance, health and fulfillment. Gathering around it meant fellowship of family and friends; and performing sacred rituals in the company of this traditional symbol of the Goddess was central to the soul-enriching Sisterhood of all Celtic women.

As an aside, the Cauldron also contributed to keeping women safe through child birth. *"How so?"* It's interesting to note that the wide-ranging use of iron in Celtic Cauldrons leached enough iron supplement into the soups and stews to bring women's iron needs up to standard. This strengthened their blood and allowed them to deliver children more safely. Other early cultures weren't as lucky, they used brass or copper pots and suffered from higher rates of infant mortality. The iron pots were also an aid to healing the warriors who had lost great quantities of blood through serious battle wounds. This hidden iron supplement was just another gift from the Goddess for honoring Her presence in their homes. Although the Celts may not have known exactly why the iron Cauldrons helped, every young woman of child-bearing age was gifted with a Cauldron of her own.

The Cauldron of Inspiration legend is important to understand, because it relates to the Shapeshifting and Invisibility part of the upcoming Banishing Ritual.

The Goddess Ceridwen boiled up a magick brew in the Cauldron of Knowledge and Inspiration. She planned to give a cup to her disadvantaged son, so that he might be struck wise. During its simmering, She summoned a young lad, Gwion, to attend the fire. While he stirred the potion, three drops slopped over the rim onto his finger, scalding it. Gwion put the finger in his mouth and sucked at the drops, thereby becoming wise himself. Ceridwen was furious. She pursued the lad relentlessly, but he avoided Her wrath by shapeshifting: changing into birds and animals and, once, a salmon. He even rendered himself invisible for a time. This boy became the famous poet and hero, Taliesin, and the three drops of Inspiration from the Cauldron became a symbol of wisdom to the Celtic sages in the earliest of times.

In this Banishing Ritual, the Cauldron of Inspiration will be your swirling herbal bath. Here you will taste of the three symbolic drops of Inspiration, in order to become altered and, in a sense, invisible to the wrath of your bad memories and sorrows. Be aware that the ritual procedures are quite different from the previous rituals, but the results will be extraordinary.

Quick Minute Magick: Banishing Your Fears and Sorrows Ritual

In this important ritual, the bathtub will be your central place of power. You may carry out this ritual in your imagination, as all the others, but you will have to pay close attention to the steps.

I don't need to remind you of the importance of using your Power Fist, casting your Spell of Protection, and the other basic elements of successful Goddess ritual. The Spell of Banishment in the ritual includes a trigger, so that you can access its powers whenever you need them in the future.

Strike up all your senses, smell the incense, feel the warm waters of the bath and inhale the steam from its aromatic herbs. Exercise your full imagination. And if you can actually soak in a hot tub while you read the ceremony, do so. It will enhance the experience even further.

Here's the list of Sacred Tools to gather in preparation for the ritual. I've included some tools for a mini-ritual to be sure you sleep well afterwards.

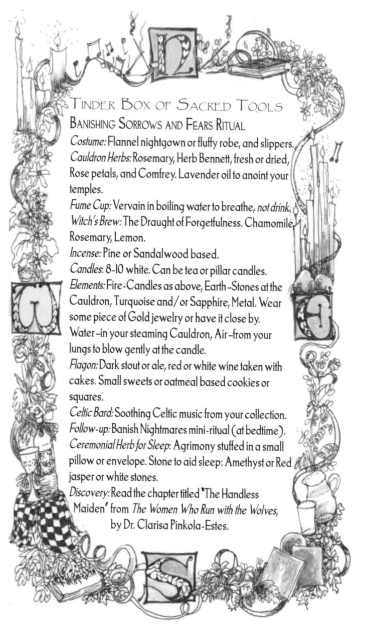

Tinder Box of Sacred Tools

Banishing Sorrows and Fears Ritual

Costume: Flannel nightgown or fluffy robe, and slippers.

Cauldron Herbs: Rosemary, Herb Bennett, fresh or dried, Rose petals, and Comfrey. Lavender oil to anoint your temples.

Fume Cup: Vervain in boiling water to breathe, *not drink.*

Witch's Brew: The Draught of Forgetfulness. Chamomile, Rosemary, Lemon.

Incense: Pine or Sandalwood based.

Candles: 8-10 white. Can be tea or pillar candles.

Elements: Fire-Candles as above, Earth-Stones at the Cauldron, Turquoise and/or Sapphire, Metal. Wear some piece of Gold jewelry or have it close by. Water-in your steaming Cauldron, Air-from your lungs to blow gently at the candle.

Flagon: Dark stout or ale, red or white wine taken with cakes. Small sweets or oatmeal based cookies or squares.

Celtic Bard: Soothing Celtic music from your collection.

Follow-up: Banish Nightmares mini-ritual (at bedtime).

Ceremonial Herb for Sleep: Agrimony stuffed in a small pillow or envelope. Stone to aid sleep: Amethyst or Red jasper or white stones.

Discovery: Read the chapter titled "The Handless Maiden" from *The Women Who Run with the Wolves,* by Dr. Clarisa Pinkola-Estes.

Significance of the Sacred Tools to the Banishing Ritual

Costume: Since the ceremony is performed in the bath, I suggest you choose a cuddly flannel nightgown, or a big thick robe and slippers as your after-the-ceremony costume. As you slip into it after your Banishing victory, imagine you are getting a great, big warm hug from the Great Mother.

Cauldron: Rosemary, also called the faery's Elfin Herb, will enhance the remembering aspects prior to your forgetting. Herb Bennett removes any vestiges of depression or despair associated with the shadows that will be swept away. Roses are known to heal the emotions, the body, and the heart. Their distinct fragrance, even when dried, is a reminder of sunny times. Use large handfuls of fresh or dried petals. Comfrey, also called Knitbone, was an effective aid in the setting of broken bones. It was also a primary herb used to ease the devastating effects of grief, to cure emotional hurts, and remove lingering scars from the heart. Lavender's properties for calming, for uplifting the spirits, for banishing darkness, and for protection are legendary. If you have essential oil, touch it to your temples and add a few drops to your bath water.

With fragrant rose petals bobbing on the bath's surface, Lavender's fragrance in the swirling steam, the healing magick of Comfrey and the protection of Herb Bennett all stirred into the comforting waters of your Cauldron—how can you fail to be blessed?

The Draught of Forgetfulness: This potion is to symbolize the ancient Druid remedy for heartache and sorrow. Brew a cup of Chamomile tea, either a bag or the loose dried flowers. When the tea is steeped to strong, remove the bag (but leave the floating flowers if that is what you used) and pour the tea into a bowl large enough to scoop both your hands into. Fill the bowl to halfway with cool water—pure spring water, if possible—and add several springs of fresh Rosemary and a few slices of lemon. Rosemary is the memory herb. It will sharpen your wits so you remember to forget. The Lemon slices are acidic and sour to wake up your senses, so you don't miss a beat. Carry the bowl to your bath and put it on the counter.

The Fume Cup: This is a special addition for this ritual. Prepare it after you prepare the bowl of the Draught of Forgetfulness. The Fume cup is simply a mug of hot water with a tablespoon of Vervain. (Use dried Vervain or the powdered capsule form.) If you can't find it, use Valerian. Both were sacred and highly regarded healing and ceremonial herbs. The ceremonial significance of Vervain (or to a lesser degree, Valerian) is major. The Celts called it "Fer Faen." It was used in divining and was considered superior for relieving serious emotional pressures and for lifting emotional pain from the soul. It had superior powers of protection and was believed to open your psychic channels to the light. Even the rules for gathering the herb were strict. It was usually harvested at the rise of the Dog Star, which came out "betwixt and between" the sun and moon. Before gathering the wild plant, a liquid libation of alcohol and honey (probably Mead) was poured on the ground near it as an offering, then the Vervain was dug up, using only the sacred hand—the left hand. It was to be kept in a specially designated leather pouch and safeguarded from negative forces. Inhaling its smoke was one of the chief methods of releasing Vervain's cosmic powers, and it was sometimes burned with a hot coal on an iron shovel. It was also mixed into a boiling cauldron, and the steam inhaled, as from your Fume Cup.

Magical stones: Semi-precious stones used for this ritual are optional, of course, but you'd be surprised how many people have some Turquoise jewelry in the bottom of their jewelry box, or a Sapphire ring their grandmother left to them. The Turquoise stone treats melancholy and restores good emotional health. All past sorrows cause some degree of melancholia. The Sapphire stone is a most powerful magick stone to reflect fears.

If many of your shadows have left you with fragments of real fears, try to borrow one for this ceremony. If you can't find either, use the Amethyst from the previous ritual or your favorite rock which has its own positive powers.

Metal: Gold should be part of your ceremony. Its luster reflects light and its patina offers deep and abiding comfort. Gold is known to open up centers for emotional healing and to welcome love. It has represented trust and loyalty and affection for centuries. In this ritual, the wealth associated with the possession of Gold means the wealth of the soul. Wear all the Gold necklaces, bracelets, or rings you can on your naked body and into your Cauldron bath.

Bard: I suggest one of the Celtic recordings used previously. The Chieftains ancient tunes in tribute to Edwin Bunting (*The Celtic Harp*), or Lorenna McKennitt's haunting songs would be suitable.

Flagon: It can be dark stout, dark ale; or red or white wine. Three sacred threads colored black, red and white were the formal ceremonial colors of the early Goddess Clans. Choose either wine color to celebrate your victory, but add the sweetness of ceremonial cakes. They can be anything you like, but a cake or cookie with oatmeal was traditional. As always, chose a natural non-alcoholic drink if it suits your beliefs, but try to pick one of the three colors. The important thing is to bring an air of celebration to mark the successful completion of your ceremonial passage.

A word about your first shapeshifting spell

There's an aspect to this ceremony that involves the Celtic act of altering your state, or shapeshifting, which in this case will mean reshaping personal history and assuming invisibility. The charm or spell to bring on shapeshifting is known as the Celtic Fith-Fath, pronounced *Fee Fie*. The spell is a simple rhyme that is said to alter or shift your consciousness is just those few words.

"Hey! 'Fee Fie' rings a distant bell!" Probably, because it's another one of your Mother Goose (Mother Goddess) nursery rhymes. Like the Lady (Goddess Epona) with rings on her fingers and bells on her toes, the Fith-Fath was part of your childhood joy. It is spoken by the giant in the tale of Jack and the Beanstalk. Incidentally, the Gaelic term for "giant" was used among the Celts to designate people of great tribal distinction, those who had attained great public admiration and stood "heads above" the common folk—not someone who was eight feet tall. In any case, the giant is repeating a version of the shapeshifting spell. It went something like this: "Fee Fie, Foe Fum. I smell the blood of an Englishman, Be he alive, or be he dead; I'll grind his bones to make me bread." Delightfully ghastly.

In your Banishment Ritual, you'll repeat the Clan Mothers' words in the shapeshifting charm, in order to disassociate yourself from your bad memories and render yourself emotionally "invisible."

Preparations for the later mini-ritual: Banishing nightmares

The mini-ritual to banish nightmares is to be done after the larger ritual when you are ready for bed. A good sound sleep, free of nightmares, will ensure success of the Banishment Rituals.

For this little ceremony you need only two things: Amethyst or Red Jasper; and a few spoonfuls of dried Agrimony stuffed in a little cloth pillow or folded into a fabric envelope (you need to be able to catch a whiff of the fragrance). Agrimony draws the nurturing comfort of deep sleep and should be placed beneath your pillow.

The Amethyst stone or Red Jasper are placed under your bed to ensure you have no nightmares. Both are excellent conductors of protection. They are known to banish nightmares and to usher in pleasant dreams, along with restful sleep.

Follow-up: I suggest you read the chapters on the Handless Maiden in the book, *Women Who Run With the Wolves*. It is the ancient tale of a woman who faces constant challenges. Like the Clan Mothers' teachings, this tale is important because it illustrates that our life is both fraught with peril and sprinkled with blessings. Read bits of it each night and imagine you are back in time, a thousand or more years ago, because stories like this were the teaching tools that prepared women for life's struggles. The Clan Mothers were fierce in their belief that a woman, thus prepared, was a woman strengthened and fortified for the journey ahead. Thanks be to Dr. Pinkola-Estes for the work she has done throughout her lifetime to unearth these wise truths, to remove cultural or religious amendments, and to pass them on so that we may benefit from the raw, elemental wisdom therein.

Steps in your Ritual of Banishment

This ritual has many steps, and you would benefit from reading through the chapter before attempting it. The entire ritual takes place in your bathroom. Celebrate later in the living room.

Set up your music and have it playing loud enough to hear in the bath (or bring it in if the machine is portable). Take eight to 10 white candles and place them right in the sink for safety if there is little room (don't light them until you return with the Fume Cup). Set up your incense, ready to light. Put your symbols of the four elements on the counter or the floor (considering that bathrooms are seldom very large, make the bath your symbol of Water since the Cauldron is central to the ritual). Hang your fuzzy sleep wear on the hook on the back of the door. Fill your tub with hot water at a temperature to soothe comfortably. Sprinkle it with the Cauldron of Inspiration herbs and strew handfuls of the flower petals on top. Rub Lavender oil on your temples, sniff it, and add a few drops to your bath. Put on all the gold jewelry you can wear. You may carry in a copy of the following Spell to Banish Fears (you should have enough light from the many candles to read it), but it would be more effective if you could memorize it in advance.

In the kitchen: Prepare your celebratory wine and cakes. Pour your red wine or juice in a nice goblet, or open your white wine and set it on ice to chill. Set your cakes on a plate. Carry to the living room.

Prepare the Draught of Forgetfulness: Boil the water, add Chamomile to a mug and steep the tea bag or loose dried flowers. When it is strong, pour it into a large bowl and add more pure water until half full. Add several sprigs of fresh Rosemary, or dried if need be. Float slices of fresh Lemon on top and bring to the bathroom.

Return to the kitchen: In another mug, stir boiling water into the dried Vervain or Valerian. Stir briskly. This Fume Cup, a version of the steam waters you inhaled in other rituals, is more potent than the Witch's Brew teas and is **not** meant to be drunk. Carry it to the bath.

Let's begin the Ritual to Banish past sorrows and shadows

You are in your bathroom. It's moist and steamy with fragrant herbs and hot water. Light all the candles. Light the incense. Take off your clothes. Leave on the gold.

Begin with the Fume Cup. Sit on the edge of your tub and inhale the steam from the potion. Cup your hand over the top of the Fume Cup to direct the steam to your nose. Inhale deeply, hold for the count of three, look away, and exhale. See the darkness leave your body on your exhaled breath. Repeat three times until the exhaled air feels light and clear. Dump the contents of the hot Fume Cup into your Cauldron of Inspiration (bath). More herbs to stir, more power within the steaming waters to heal and comfort you.

Stand in the center of the room and make your Power Fist, say, "Mother-Mine," out loud as the tingling energy of the Goddess within surges up your arm and fills your being. Cast your Spell of Protection. The misty luminous light surrounds and protects you. Stand tall and call upon the Goddess to attend you. Speak to Her of your hopes to clear away those sorrows and hurts that have haunted you, to come to terms with the shadows that continue to impose themselves upon you. Blow softly on the candles and be aware of their luminous magick. Know that the warm air of your lungs, the same air that the Clan Mothers breathed so many centuries ago, is part of the magick that is you. Cast your Golden Circle of Light around yourself and the steaming Cauldron beside you. Call on the energies of the four compass points, the Airts, and bid them genuine welcome to attend your ritual.

Now call upon your Spirit Guides to help you through this ritual. Call them by name and ask that all the guides, all your loving ancestors, all the entities assigned to you, be present to help support you in this healing ceremony. Say aloud, "Blessed be, Great Mother. I am never alone."

Now go to the bowl holding the Draught of Forgetfulness. Lean over it, and say, "Great Mother, as the hero Cuchullin benefited from the healing waters of the Draught of Forgetfulness, so bless me this night. And, as the hand of the wise Druidess scooped the waters to mend his heartache, Great Mother, heal me and make me whole again."

Brush aside the fruit and flowers floating on the surface of your Draught of Forgetfulness. With your cupped left hand, scoop up the liquid and drink from your hand. Do it three times. Then, hold your empty cupped hand over your mouth and nose and breathe in once. Say, "Let the cupped hand of the ancient Druidess serve as my trigger; that I may, ever after, have the magick power to remember to forget all that I leave behind this night."

Pour the contents of the bowl into your bath, and say, "Blessed be, this gift of forgetting."

Step into your bath and sink into the waters. Have the Spell to Banish fears close at hand. Once you are relaxed, you're going to taste of the three Drops of Inspiration from your Cauldron of Inspiration; to tap into that ancient power of wisdom, inspiration, and understanding. Dip your finger in the bath water and let a single drop roll off the end of your finger and into your mouth. Say, "By the Grace of the Goddess within me, I drink in Women's Power."

Dip your finger again. Let another drop fall into your mouth and say, "By the enduring traditions of the learned Druidess, I drink in Women's Magick."

Once more, after the third drop say, "By the blessings of the circle of loving Clan Mothers, I drink in Women's Wisdom."

Now lie back in the warm waters and stare at the space or the wall before you. This is where you are going to run a mental movie of the scenes from your past sorrows and dark shadows. Say this only once, "Great Mother-Mine, let the good of these lessons remain to serve me; let their pain vanish forevermore."

Here is a summary of what happens next: Before you project the first mental movie segment from your past shadows, you must first disassociate yourself emotionally. You will see yourself as the star in the scene, but your soul will be absent from the pain of it all. You will shapeshift. You will make yourself emotionally invisible; you will be a casual observer, sitting in the audience with no attachment whatsoever to the person or event on the screen. You are lying in the comfort of your Cauldron of Inspiration, watching the movie without emotion. If you find yourself beginning to get upset, squeeze your Power First again and say Mother-Mine out loud. You will be strengthened, and your inner self will be removed from the feelings and reactions this unhappy scene caused you.

When you have seen enough, you will say the Spell to Banish Fears with rhythm and conviction. As you finish, the movie will begin to fade, break into misty fragments, and drift off—up and away—while you remain safe and comfortable in the warm waters of the Goddess' Cauldron.

You are ready, dear friend. If you wish, make your Power Fist once again under water. Squeeze it tight to remember how magical you are, how strong you have become. Okay, let's do it. But just before you run the first sorrowful movie scene, say the shapeshifting Celtic charm:

Fee Fie, Fee Fie.
Render me Invisible to this sorrowful past.

You will not be a part of the mental movie. You will see yourself, but you are safely outside those terrible happenings. Totally disassociated. Totally unemotional. Pain free. Take a second to be aware of yourself in the tub, splash the water with your hand—it is not you up on your movie screen.

Run the first scene, one from your childhood. There may be no sound, or low sound. The movie isn't bright, the picture is dull and muddy. You know how it goes. You've run that very scene a million times in your mind and suffered each and every time. When you have seen enough, say this most effective Spell to Banish Fears taken from Jeni Couzyn's book, *House of Changes*:

By the warmth of the sun
By the baby's cry
By the lambs on the hill
I banish Thee
By the sweetness of the song
By the warm rain falling
By the hum of the grass
Begone.

Imagine the scene dulling down, as if the lights are failing, browning out. Watch as the final still scene breaks apart, as the fragments drift off. The last tiny bits float to the ceiling and disappear. Cup your hand over your mouth and breathe. This is your trigger to forgetting. The value of the lesson remains, but the sorrowful memory is gone. It will trouble you no more. Say, "Blessed be."

Project the next scene of sorrow, fear or pain. Repeat the steps: Power Fist; Shapeshifting charm; disassociate yourself from the person in the movie scene. Run the dull movie. Watch without emotion. Repeat the words of the Spell to Banish Fears. Freeze the last frame. Watch without feeling as it breaks apart, drifts up and away. When it's gone, make the Draught of Forgetfulness gesture as your trigger for this bad memory as well. (You may use this trigger gesture any time unwanted memories try to creep back into your thoughts. Simply cup your hand and say, "Begone." It works.)

Do as many as you wish. One after the other: disassociated from your feelings; faded in importance; stripped of all power over you; and finally banished, once and for all. You'll get more efficient and faster as you work through your sorrows.

When you find you are growing tired, **stop.** If you have more sorrows to deal with, do them another time. **Don't let yourself get weary or depleted in any way.** Even if you banish but one haunting memory in this ritual, you are ahead on the scoreboard. Be good to yourself.

When you are finished and ready to get out and close your ritual, make the Power Fist and say, "Great Mother, fill up the void with happiness and joy. Merry Merry Meet."

Now it is time to climb out of the tub, wrap in a towel, and close your ritual the same way you always have. Thank the Airts and release them; thank the Goddess and ask for Her blessing on you; and close your Golden Circle counter-clockwise. Then whoop and jump and make a joyful noise. Dry off with gusto. Wrap yourself in the warmth of your thick robe or fuzzy nightclothes. Give yourself a hug.

Take one candle and the incense for the trip to the living room. Blow out the rest of the candles. Scoop out the herbs and pull the plug on your bath. Head for the living room and the awaiting wine and cakes. Yahoo, time to celebrate! Put some dancing music on the stereo and dance about. Don't you feel lighter and brighter? That was quite an experience! Banishments are always life-altering rituals. If you feel a bit shaky, carry the Amethyst around while you dance, or hold your favorite rock close to your heart. Eat lots of yummy sweet cakes. It's a party! A farewell party to all those things you should have said goodbye to years ago.

And it's a celebration! A welcoming celebration for all the wonderful opportunities and events and people and ideas and joys that are coming to fill up that freshly-vacated space in your soul. That empty place is already flooding with sunlight, and there's new paint and brass fixtures and gold-plated taps in the bath and goodness knows what else! Room to rent—no triflers need apply.

Banishing nightmares mini-ritual

There's just one more step, a kind of final closure. Consider it cosmic insurance. Personal property (your soul) insurance. You see, most of your pain has been festering away at the subconscious or soul level. It mostly seeps into your conscious thoughts when you are tired, or not paying attention. Or your subconscious hijacks your dreamtime and fills it with nightmares whenever it feels a bit mischievous. So, as an added precaution after all the fine healing work you've done, you will address this dreaming part of yourself directly, so everything is in harmony.

When you go to bed, place the Amethyst or Red Jasper under your bed. If you have neither, use your favorite rock, since we know it is already charged with concern and care for you. Now, place the little cloth pillow or envelope of Agrimony under your own sleeping pillow; or put the dried herb in a bowl beside the bed and bruise it between your fingers while you breathe in its protective fragrance. If you can't find Agrimony, make up a bowl of fool-proof kitchen protection: Basil, Rosemary, Chervil, and Chamomile. It will help protect you from nightmares.

> *In Celtic legend, there are many examples of the Death Crone (or Demon Crone) who rides out at night to visit those with a bad conscience and terrorizes them with unsettling dreams. Since the early Celts believed the Goddess knew everything, it made sense that She knew of a person's deepest fears and most hidden, sorrowful secrets. The names of these many faces of the Goddess are varied throughout history, but often they translate as "the black horse" or "one who rides the Night Mare."*

It's worth examining your nightmares closely to determine whether they are trying to tell you something. Perhaps you need to rectify an unresolved issue or relationship. Consider seeking or granting forgiveness, or making amends for any harm done to someone, even if it was unintentional. Setting it right may also resolve your nightmare issues. Cleanse yourself and forgive yourself. Call on your inner Goddess and create a restful sleep, so you can boogie-on-down your path of joy.

Make your Power Fist and ask, "Great Mother-Mine, hold me in the protection of your arms this and every night."

Cup your hand over your mouth and whisper, "That I may evermore remember to forget." Now, read the Spell to Banish Nightmares. While you do so, draw the outline of a capital G on your forehead several times with your finger:

> **Great Mother-Mine, hear my plea**
> **Make my dreams nightmare free**
>
> **Unleash no carnage, no frightful scare**
> **Grab up the reins, hold back the black mare**
>
> **Nightmares take heed from wisdom beyond**
> **Depart with speed when you hear my sweet song.**
>
> **Vanish all nightmares**
> **Nightmares Begone.**

Turn out the light with calm confidence. You have earned it. Think of fields of flowers and the sweet faces of loved ones. Recall holding kittens or puppies, the look of newborn colts or baby lambs. Conjure up your Nemeton. Go there and relax. Drift softly into dreamland. Sleep like a tired little toddler at the end of a long active day—a happy day. Rest your bones, like the weary wisewoman you are fast becoming—a true master of destiny; a healer of old pains; a dreamer, cast adrift among the warm breezes of the starry heavens. It doesn't get much better than that, sweet soul.

What Do I Want

Chapter Seven

Getting What You Desire From Life

The Celts believed that you chose your life before you were born. You made a pact with the Goddess to learn certain lessons for your soul's growth while you walked the face of Abred. Once here, you would be confronted with a variety of challenges so that you might learn those life lessons. For the most part, how you handled the challenges and how you went about your daily life was in your control. It was a part of the exercise of your own free will.

The Clan Mothers also taught women to think long and hard about their lives and where they wanted to go on this particular earthly journey, in order to fulfill their agreement with the Great Mother and to satisfy their soul's longing. Tribal women had to become crystal clear on what they wanted to achieve during this incarnation—a major task in and of itself. Education was of the utmost importance, but learning to concentrate and to control your thoughts and memories was considered imperative as well. Self control, positive thinking, and faith in yourself were essential to proceed into the world with resolute certainty and assurance. With each step taken in confidence, the success of the venture was guaranteed.

Today, the same code for living applies. The Goddess is here to be sure that whatever you tell Her you desire will come to you. That seems terrific. There is only one snag. You have to be extremely clear on what you want and what you desire, or you'll mangle the message and give self-canceling instructions. Learning to know what you want is a difficult part of the equation. Learning to phrase it in your mind with complete clarity and positive affirmation is yet another challenge. Once you master the inner communications with the Goddess, everything you desire will come to you.

I've included an exercise to help determine what is important to you, and where you'd like your path to lead. You'll discover how to visualize your ideal life so it may become reality, and learn a bardic chant of affirmation to keep your confidence high. Once you know your desired destination, getting there is easy.

Understanding the Celtic Web of Life

The ancient Celts believed all life was intertwined and humans were only part of this great complicated Web of Life. They accepted that their destiny was part fate, part choice. The Clan Mothers believed in cycles of life based on their reverence and understanding of nature. Great Moon watchers, they were well aware that women's menstrual cycles were tied to the waxing and waning of the moon's 28-day cycle. They monitored the changes within their bodies and realized that energy was strongest at certain times of the month cycle, and emotions were either calm or confused at others. Even clarity of thought became an issue at certain times of the month.

And women were keenly aware of the tides of their own sexual desire, that peaked or waned as the changing face of Mother Moon traveled across the starry skies. They celebrated and revered the passing of the seasons—the yearly cycles of warmth, brightness, joy and abundance, followed with reliable certainty of darkness, cold, isolation, and the anxiety caused by dwindling supplies.

They understood and made allowance for these internal and external changes, embracing the roller coaster of life's cycles as an intrinsic foundation of their faith. And they were ever aware of the code of living as taught by the early Druidic sages, which continued to be passed on by the Clan Mothers after most Druids had been killed by the Romans. The code outlined the holy three-fold principle that all people must accept as our human conditions here on Abred. I'll list them, for they clearly show where you have options in life, and where you do not—an important distinction:

1. The necessity to suffer.
2. The necessity to accept change.
3. The importance of choice, or the exercise of free will.

What does this have to do with getting what you want in life? Plenty. You just need to understand where and how you can exercise your gift of free will—then go for it. Accept what cannot be changed, that is, the challenges you must meet up to, then, with the rest, create a custom-designed and fulfilling life by waving the wand of your magick, your own far-reaching free will.

Acknowledging the necessity to suffer in life

"*C.C., didn't we get caught in this particular revolving door in the last chapter?*" Yes, we did, but perhaps it needs just a bit more attention. Let's focus on this: the Clan Mothers taught that suffering is a given that must be accepted; yet, at the same time, it is a beautiful gift.

It's a practical point of view. Suffering has always been a part of our lives—the bottom of the circle—or as the Clan Mothers called it the dark of the moon. Those times when there's no moon at all—just the dark of it—when the Goddess is off exploring the Underworld, and you may feel as if you're left to cope with your life challenges all alone. Just remember, you made those learning arrangements before you came to Abred; your only task here is to learn all you can from the challenges you face, and to endure. When all the good has been squeezed from an experience, you must let it go as you learned in the past chapter. And if the burden is self-inflicted, or thrown over your shoulders by family or society, bid it farewell as you did in Chapter Four, "Breathing life into your soul." When it comes to life's harsher lessons, follow this code: study, glean the positive instruction, be aware of all that occurred, then dump it in the trash can of experience and move on—lighter, wiser, and full of delightful expectation.

Accepting and embracing change in your life

Change is the middle principle for a reason: it is influenced both by the lessons learned through suffering, and by the forceful exercise of our own free will. The Clan Mothers would say, "Dear Clan Daughter, learn to cope with the many challenges of change. Get good at it, for change is inevitable. It comes from without, and from within yourself. Accept it. Embrace it. Wrap your arms around change, and balance will come to your life."

Change presents itself every time a friend or loved one moves in and out of our lives. It is woven into the three faces of the Goddess, the three major phases of life: the Maiden, the Mother, and the Wise Crone. Consider the bodily and emotional changes that take us from infancy to puberty, they are so overwhelming that, looking back, they are almost beyond understanding—wow, did all that happen to me? Then we become mothers, we birth our children or the creative endeavors of our soul work, or both. We love and lose love. Our parents grow old. We in turn grow old. And all the while, the vortex of change is swirling through the world around us: pestilence, war, famine, death—all the fun stuff—not to mention changing technology and trends. Whew! It's a wonder we can cope at all.

We can and do. We endure and come to know the divine within us. The sum total of our experiences, those cases of intuitive knowing and shared compassion, begin to tally up on the plus side of life's ledger, to spill slowly over into the realm of women's wisdom. At the time, you don't even realize the Goddess is dancing you toward that state of blissful wisdom, of women's knowing. But you begin, through a combination of suffering and accepting change, to understand. To truly understand.

Those are the two heavy "necessities." The "life's a long, muddy road" part of the equation. *"So, what about 'free will?'"* It's the part that's been languishing in a dark corner somewhere, while you've felt buffeted about by life, enjoying it at times but, mostly, it just seems to be slipping through your cosmic fingers and spilling out all over the dark soil of Abred. In accepting the principles of suffering and change, you feel as if everything in life is imposed on you from external sources, and must be accepted stoically. Hey, wake up! You do have some control.

Happily taking charge of the free will component in your life

You've known a few thrilling moments when you felt you had made a choice, but it likely didn't last very long before you felt swept away by circumstances, by random occurrences and events beyond your control. Well, you're partially right. Those life challenges you negotiated as a spirit are headed your way—come hell or high water, as they say. But the Goddess is compassionate. She allows you time between lessons to rest, to enjoy and to—hear this word, because it's crucial—*direct* the unfolding of your life. To exercise your *free will*. This is the high point of the circle, the full moon's silvery glow. The "sex, drugs, and rock 'n' roll" option, if you are so inclined.

You've exercised this ancient Celtic principle a number of times already. You chose to go on to higher education, or not. You chose a mate and married him, and stayed with him, or not. You embarked on a career with a single vision of success, or not. You chose to get pregnant at exactly the right time for you, or not—get the drift? These are natural points in your life where you were the captain of your ship, and you piloted it or chose to let it founder. It was your choice, and whether you let others make the decision for you, or not—well, my friend, you were exercising choice then, too.

And you have known the thrill of making up your own mind. Of making your own choice—sink or swim. It was your well thought-out decision, or maybe a heartfelt one, even if it didn't appear to have a lot of merit to others at the time. And wasn't it fun? At the very least, it was "butterflies in the stomach" exciting, wasn't it?

But here's the problem. After those key decisions were made, you probably gave up the captain routine and drifted aimlessly or, worse yet, experienced a shipwreck of sorts. What you didn't know, was what the Clan Mothers taught young women: you have to continue to hold tight to the ship's wheel; you must chart the course and navigate your own voyage of self-discovery. That's why confidence and a strong dollop of self-esteem were woven into a Clan daughter's self-image, starting in her formative years. It allowed her to make the natural move to becoming the captain of her own destiny. It's your life—steer it in whatever direction you choose. Sure, storms will buffet you as you ride out a tidal wave of life lessons; and, yes, things beyond your control will sometimes send you back to the map to quickly alter course but, all-in-all, you are in charge. It's your excellent adventure.

I don't have to mention that you'll have to make compromises based on personal relationships, or that you will occasionally hitch your ship to another for some years of smooth sailing—or a promise of such—this happens from time to time. We are women. Nurturers. We know about making allowances, about sometimes deciding to put our personal aspirations on temporary hold. Accepted. It's a fact of life. But listen up! Hear the stern voices of the Clan Mothers echoing down through time's tunnel: never leave your station at the ship's wheel; never, *ever*, relinquish your rightful hold on your own free will. If the need arises, reach over with your sharp ceremonial dagger and cut the stout line that joins you to the other ship. Exercising your rights is never easy. But it is essential to know that at any given time, you can crank that wheel to the left, turn the nose of your lovely little vessel into the wind, and speed off in a more favorable direction. Wave good-bye. Blow kisses from the bridge. Love you. Catch you later. I'm off.

Where to now, you daring adventurer? You've made the big move to take back yourself in some major way—to free yourself physically, emotionally, intellectually, or financially. Whatever. The wild seas await you; the salt breeze is tingling your skin and ruffling your hair; and you can breathe strong, breathe fresh, breathe free.

As usual, the Clan Mothers had three essential elements for designing a life based on spiritual, practical, and magical considerations. Here they are with more explanation following:

1. Call on spiritual guidance to sort out what you really desire.
2. Emphasize the practical: preparation is everything.
3. Master the magical process of creative visualization and affirmation.

Sorting through the possibilities for enriching your life is a daunting task. As such, it's a natural place to call on spiritual guidance to help steer you through the forest of desires. In the past, had you lived in the time of the Clan of the Goddess, you would simply have gone to the Council of Old Women for such specialized help and advice. Why? Well, they were wise for one, having survived past menopause; and they were skilled in divination, so they could call on the spirits for key direction. Surprise! You've learned to do that yourself, haven't you? You're well on your way to becoming a Clan Mother yourself.

Traditional role of the Clan Mothers in designing your life

The nature of the Clan Mothers' tribal responsibility made it easy for them to help guide a young women through many life choices. Besides, they had watched her intently from infancy, at play with all the other tribal children, and during her interaction with peers and adults. They were mindful of her attachment to animals or nature; and they were carefully observant of her body, and the strengths and weaknesses it revealed as she grew. Her progress during childhood instruction was monitored closely. Aptitude in specific subjects or ease at learning certain skills was duly noted, as it would indicate the child's budding preferences and talents, as well as her developing character.

In addition to watching her grow and develop certain interests, the Clan Mothers kept the child's parentage in the back of their minds, and were mindful of any good or bad signs that may have been inherited—in personality and intellect; or in physical, mental, emotional and spiritual abilities. Although all professions in the tribal system were open to either men or women, they realized that such traits as leadership, learning, or animal husbandry were often influenced by the professions or skills of the adults in their household. Determining suitability to various occupations was a serious task, since many vocations and professions required a person with specialized skills or talents or innate gifts. A large, self-sufficient tribe might be wealthy enough to support a number of artisans and crafts people, as well as medical specialists, educators, and priestesses. There was a full range of options from swine herder to healer, chief to midwife, potter to administrator. Regardless of the final choice, every young person was expected to play a role in the support and sustenance of their tribe and village; ideally one that was also satisfying and ultimately rewarding to the young person.

So, when you requested a special council with the Clan Mothers to help chart your life's course, they were ready with a great number of possibilities to lay at your feet. They'd toss the colored divining bones, or throw a handful of fern seeds over the calm surface of a Cauldron to seek spiritual guidance for you. Then they'd help you look into your heart for what your soul was saying, for what it would take to make it happy during this incarnation on Abred. Once decided, your schedule for education through fosterage, or through intensive training, inside or outside the tribe, was arranged and, if need be, funded from the collective coffers of the Celts social service monies. That made life a lot easier to design, didn't it?

But still, you didn't relinquish control to the wisewomen. Nor were you stuck on one career path if it didn't suit you. The Clan Mothers were highly cognizant of how important it was that you flourished in your decided life path. If you didn't, it was obviously the wrong one and adjustments were made. They knew a happy woman was a confident woman, and her best work would be done in the areas that made her most joyful.

Ah, but what about love? Whom would you love? When and how many children would you bear, or later accept and love as foster children under your training? Would you stay with the tribe? What other skills or arts would you take up to enrich your life further? What friends would form your loving, protective circle? Though your training or job might furnish some of the answers, you still had the free will to choose and to act. Then, as now, you could still formulate the details, and choose the people and opportunities that you wanted to fill your life.

Decide what you fancy from life

What do I desire in my life? Sounds easy. Well, my friend, it is. Simply ask yourself this: **If I could have anything I want in life, no matter the cost or the seeming impossibility, what would it be?** No restrictions, now. No obstacles. What would your ideal life look like? Who would be in it? Where would you live? What would you be doing? I'd wager a velvet bag full of golden coins that you have absolutely no trouble coming up with the ideal picture. No restrictions? Easy. You know exactly what you'd be doing. Right? Me, too.

Close your eyes for a moment. Make your personal Power Fist. Cast your Spell of Protection around you and call on your Spirit Guide to be with you.

Now, tell me, what would such a life look like? Dream big. Hold nothing back. Speak it aloud. Savor all the delicious details. It'll come to you—fast and furious—because until now, you have been operating on the wrong plane. You've been living a life filled with limitations, constraints, and all the extraneous rules that say "No." It's been a life lived in a box, and I'll bet it hasn't been a very big, or a very satisfying or exciting box at that.

Now, let's look at each one of the "restrictions" that stop you from having or doing the ideal things—the things you easily recognized as making you happy. Why? Because you should be doing exactly what you just described. That ideal life should be your real life. The obstacles that keep you from it should be removed, circumvented, or knocked over. You should have what you desire.

Not enough money to go back to university and study anthropology, medicine, or religion? Get the catalog and circle the courses you want. Talk to a student counselor. Get all set to go and the funding will fall into place. A leap of faith? You bet. But wallowing in self-pity while pursuing an uninspiring life isn't an easy job, either. Be confident your dreams will come true. Start down the path and success will find you.

Can't afford to move away from the subsidized urban housing that's dangerous and threatening to you and your children? Find a way. Move to a small house, in a small town, with low rents and safe streets. With a community to call your own. Start over. What housing did you picture? Find a way to get it. Tired of the dirty city? Start looking at country places, right now. Have no money? Don't worry, begin the search anyway. If you have truly decided that country living will enrich your dull and depressing life, then that, my friend, is your life path. If it will make you happier, do it. Be confident that the ways and means will be found. Money is one of the easiest things to manifest. The hard thing is being clear about what you need it for, being clear about what you really desire. Open your heart and soul and dream big.

Call on your Spirit Guide, your guardian angel, your ancestors and entities to help you make it happen. Talk to them, as you would a circle of influential friends with deep pockets. Decide. Plan. Watch it all begin to happen. What do you have to lose? The exercise alone will add spice to your life.

Preparation is everything

Look at your progress so far. You've called on your spirit helpers for assistance and decided what you want, no restrictions. Now you need to add a little elbow grease: preparation is everything.

Obviously, your preparation varies according to your selected life plan or lifestyle. Let's assume you want to move to

Mexico and live near the ocean in a warm, tropical paradise. That's your unequivocal dream. That would make you most happy. So the restrictions to overcome are money, language, family you don't want to leave or disappoint, and on and on. Forget the downers. Start planning as if it's a "go." Do your action-planning part of the bargain.

Get literature on different places; go to the library; get on the Internet and find out the living details: housing, health care, visas, etc. Join a chat line of expatriates who could become your friends. Cost out the air flights; estimate the monthly and annual cost of living; check possible funds you could access like life insurance, savings, retirement funds. Start Spanish lessons at the high school at night; join a friendship circle for new Mexican immigrants; get cook books and start making the food in your kitchen. Get some Mexican music and listen to it in the car, in your home, and while you soak in your Cauldron full of herbs that ensure success. Make it your mission. Your obsession.

Then get more practical. Save enough to take a short vacation down there and see for yourself. If it still fits, if it feels right. Go home, sell everything, and do it. Put some money aside to fly your loved ones down at Christmas. Do whatever you have to do in order to remove the restrictions. Once you begin to explore the details of your dream—the mechanics of making it happen—surprises will pop up. Maybe a charming elderly woman needs a companion and will actually pay you to live there. Or maybe it's more affordable than you assumed. Maybe retiring early does not have as many penalties as you thought it did. Anything can happen when you seriously explore the details, the possibilities.

As an aside, if Mexico's your destination, take your familiar, your beloved pet. Despite what many books say, they are allowed and even welcomed there. If your destination is England, arrange for the pet to go to the continent first and travel over with a resident of the EEC—otherwise your pet will be quarantined for six terrible months. These are the sort of details you'll learn once you throw yourself into your fact finding mission with determination.

But, you get my picture. Your spirit friends are working on one level; your confidence is doing some miraculous things on another level; and your preparedness, your action part of the bargain, is moving slowly but surely down that dream life path, until it looks like a real possibility. Next thing you know, you're on your way.

Mastering manifestation and creative visualization

Creative visualization is a tried and true technique to aid you in getting what you want—no, scratch that word—what you **desire**. What is it? It is a highly regimented practice of training your imagination to create. It is self-discipline to control your thinking and focus on your desired outcome. Since everything and everyone is energy, clear visualization techniques are most effective for telling the universe what it should do for you. How it can successfully serve you in your exercise of free will. As we discussed earlier, your imagination is one of the functions that spring from the soul, so creative visualization is direct soul work.

"And why did you cross out the word 'want' above?" Because it can be misunderstood by the energy forces that are there to serve you and help make your dreams come true. To "want" means to desire, yes, but it also means "to be impoverished" and that negative connotation is the last thing you should be putting forth in your quest to create your free will life. My mother used to say, and you've probably heard this line, "I want never gets." It was usually in response to my wishful thinking or lists upon lists of what I wanted in my young life.

But she was right. To be in a state of want does not produce results, it clouds the issue and confuses everyone concerned.

So be clear in visualizing all the details of your desired lifestyle, then think of it in terms of the present. Not, "I *hope* to move to Mexico." No. Tell yourself, "I live a happy, fulfilling and socially exciting life in Mexico. All is well in my world." Simply adjust your words in order to place yourself in a cosmic position of power and confidence; a position that affirms the power of your imagination to create. First you think it—that's always the case with everything you do—then it can happen. Think in the present, then make it real with your positive affirmations.

The steps to creative visualization

The practice of creative visualization has been around for centuries. The Clan Mothers used to send young women out to the stiles to visualize their future lover.

Stiles are the steps set or carved into rock walls so people could climb over the wall to get to the next pasture, yet the cattle or other livestock couldn't escape. Stiles are steeped in myth and were often considered sacred because they served as a passage, a symbolic place that was "betwixt and between" this world and the Otherworld. Crossroads were another example of two worlds, two planes of consciousness, coming together. Ancient crossroads were thought to hold great energetic power and were honored with shrines, often erected to commemorate a person or great event in Celtic history. Stiles, set as they were in quiet pastoral settings, were considered an excellent dreaming place.

After a Celtic lass had been initiated into the tribe as a woman, she was often sent to sit on the steps of a stile, to visualize the face of the one she would come to love the most. Since marriage was a later reaction to the newer faiths, a woman often had several lovers. Still, there was usually one who would capture her heart like no other. Here, in the sacred dreaming place, she would use an early form of creative visualization, blending the elements of hope and desire with spiritual divination.

Affirmations, repeated positive invocations describing all the heart could long for, are echoes of the individual chants young Celtic women sang as they worked. My younger daughter is an adherent to the practice of affirmations; she swears they have changed her life for the better, and they absolutely contributed to the miraculous healing of a dear relative who suffered from what was considered an incurable disease. My daughter's vigilance in setting aside time to "do her affirmations" was the most important ingredient in that family miracle. Affirmations also calm her, and give her peace in her heart. Since she has a very stressful, but most satisfying creative career, those repeated affirmations have proven essential to maintaining her emotional and physical good health.

Though there have been countless books written on the subject, the best and clearest is an old one called *Creative Visualization* by Shakti Gawain that first appeared in the 1970s. It is a small book, well worth adding to your library. You'll be an expert when you finish it. In the meantime, here are the four basic steps to doing your own brand of Celtic visualization chants or affirmations.

Celtic visualization ritual

As with all rituals, make your Power Fist and give yourself a moment to feel the energy of the divine soaring through your arm and body. See it. Feel it. Cast your Spell of Protection so the light surrounds you, and call on the Goddess to ask Her to attend you. All that can be done within a few seconds, but it puts you in an altered state of mind and signals to the Forces of Good to be alert to your requests. Now paint the picture of your heart's desires—with bold colors and vivid detail.

The process for creative visualization is as follows:

1. Be very clear what your goal is, or what it is you wish to draw to your life. This could be a small thing such as a material possession, or an improved relationship, or even the complete life plan you have been working towards.

2. Quickly imagine a clearly detailed picture of that goal. The more often you do this, the easier it will be to bring such a picture forward.

3. Repetition makes perfect. Every new skill you learn—piano, driving, or skiing—needs the application of continued repetition until it is a smooth and automatic response within your mind and body. As with the skill of typing, speed and accuracy improve with practice until you can make your fingers fly at will without even thinking. At the start, practice the visualization on a daily basis or at any moment of quiet time.

4. Employ your affirmations in order to boost the strength of the positive energy. Chant or say a positive statement you have prepared. Be sure the structure of the affirmations have you enjoying

your results in the present, and never use the word "want." Picture yourself already living with the results of your creative visualization in colorful and vivid detail.

Use your personally designed affirmations, or chant a spell of creation something like this:

> **I am the Goddess shining bright**
> **I spread my life feast before me**
> **I stand and smile in Her fair light**
> **Embracing the abundance I see**
> **All I create this night is good.**
> **All I create this night is right.**
> **Mother-Mine**
> **Blessed be.**

"Do I have to visualize one thing at a time?" (Because if you are just starting to practice your gift of free will, of visualizing desires into reality, then you may indeed have a very long list.) The answer is no. Go for all of it. The whole kit 'n' caboodle. The whole magilla. See yourself with everything your heart desires. Follow the steps the Clan Mothers taught: call on your spiritual helpers; take practical steps to make your dreams happen; and use chants or creative visualization to project your fondest wishes into your real future.

Drink the roses and smell the wine

Gotcha! That's just a joke. Something to grab your attention and keep you sharp. What I want to stress is that charming Celtic habit of celebrating. Like the word "want," celebrate has two meanings that are equally important to the Celtic traditions. To celebrate means to "honor someone or something."

It also means to "cut up, make merry, and have a grand old time." Both are fitting.

We've happily included an element of joyful celebration after each personal spiritual achievement in this little book. But I may not have emphasized it enough, for the success of each component of your practice of free will should be complemented and raised up to a position of honor through celebration. Yes, by *smelling* the roses along the way and *drinking* the wine.

I don't know if this applies to you, but I have a number of otherwise enlightened friends who, once they have achieved something great, simply smile, and nod and—oh no—go headlong into expressing worries about their new future. My son, at the age of eight or nine, when presented with a new plan or change in plans would immediately ask: "Yeah but, what if... ." He did it so often, always anticipating some imagined disaster, that he was unable to appreciate the good news part in the change of plans. We gently teased him out of it, until he put it away and began to look at life more positively. Some people never leave the "what if" stage in their development. They forget to celebrate. How sad.

No doubt this new approach to designing your life, to really practicing the Goddess gifts of free will and choice, will reap amazing results, benefits, and unimagined delights. Embrace the Celtic traditions. Celebrate each little scrap of good news along the way, each minor achievement, and all the major ones. Have fun, kick up your heels, go to a movie with someone who's surprised you asked, bake a cake, buy a new puppy or kitten, call a long-neglected friend, have a drink, make some great food, and by all means, light some candles and give thanks. Then make a toast to yourself and your achievement—the wonder of getting back in touch with yourself. And give yourself the pleasure of that old Gaelic greeting of, "A hundred thousand hugs." Zippity doo-dah! Hug yourself hard. You're walking on the sunny side of the street. And you are nothing short of brilliant, for you are putting your personal magick to very practical use.

Chapter Eight

Upping the Volume on Your Laughter

Laughter isn't just for fun, it's good medicine for your soul.

The Great Mother's lessons are all about taking care of yourself—physically and spiritually—and laughter is high on Her list. Even though the early Celts lived with one foot in the Otherworld, they firmly believed you had to enjoy everything that Abred, the earthplane, offered while you were here. Laughter was essential to making their sometimes harsh and primitive world more bearable. And if you are a Celt, or know any (remember they settled in Spain, France, and other parts of Europe, as well as the British Isles), then you are aware that they can always rouse a smile, no matter the situation at hand. Humor, and the silly antics that cause us to laugh, lighten everything and everyone. Are you letting a good dose of laughter into your everyday life?

Chances are, you're walking around in a stressful daze—a permanent frown on your face, lines etched across your furrowed brow. Life is hard. Life is competitive and serious. I agree. And it's also woefully short of real laughter. Truth be known, you could use a lot more fun in your life.

Fun and frivolity—part of Celtic life

When the Celts gathered around their bonfires in the evenings, an instant party erupted. They had contests to see who could laugh the loudest and longest, tell the most amusing yarn, or sing a ditty faster than anyone else. And maybe they'd have someone stand up and recite a poem—backwards. It was all ridiculously childish, but hilarious. They'd start laughing and teasing each other as soon as they spread their animals skins on the ground near the fire's warmth. Daily life could prove hard some years—food may be scarce or war might threaten—but for a few short hours, sitting bathed in golden firelight under a blanket of twinkling stars, or under Mother Moon's silvery cloak, they'd allow themselves some delightful, and much needed, comic relief.

I once worked with a woman called Dilly. It was a fitting nickname. She was an intelligent and capable executive, someone you could rely on to get a job done well. A second generation Celt, she was blessed with that enviable gift of the bard—she could bring anyone to gales of laughter with her real-life stories. A belly laugh should be called a "Dilly," for it was her natural specialty. Let me tell you a story of the importance of humor—it doesn't have to be sophisticated. Naive and childish will do every bit as well.

Once, when a prominent dignitary decided to visit our university campus at a moment's notice, my staff was sent scrambling to arrange the extensive and highly detailed protocol and security. With major media coming, and all the arrangements to be made, we were stressed to the limit. In the emergency planning meeting to pull it all together, tension was high, the stakes even higher. While I was in the middle of assigning tasks with machine-gun rapidity, Dilly suddenly coughed twice into her hand. Suddenly, everyone turned away from me. When they turned back, my entire staff sported a red foam clown's nose! I was startled for only a heartbeat before I collapsed with laughter. All the self-imposed stress disappeared instantaneously. Although we still took the job seriously, we stopped taking ourselves that way. We staged a flawless event. We were heroes. And we had fun.

Silly? Slapstick? You bet. It was utterly ridiculous and inappropriate in the setting, but the child in me roared with delight. In a flash, I was reminded how much I was living in my mind and ignoring the joy of my soul. Years later, when I saw the Robin Williams' movie, *Patch*, I could understand the healing magick of clown noses and buffoonery. Why? Because comedy works. It delights. Admit it, you'd like to laugh more. It can happen. Let's go stir some up.

Social lives of the children of the Clan of the Goddess

Women in early times, under the loving and protective eye of the Great Mother, enjoyed themselves immensely. For centuries, they celebrated so many festivals, feasts, and ceremonial events that seldom a fortnight passed between. Some of the major festivals, like the Beltaine, included a night of relaxed sexual rules with much dancing, drinking, and letting loose. There were eight of these major festivals, called *sabbats*, held during the year, and many had to be incorporated into Christian tradition because the people refused to give them up. A recent poll showed that the sabbat known for centuries as Samhain (pronounced sow-in) is, by far, the very favorite festival of children everywhere as they gleefully dress up in wild costumes like the ancient Mummers. It's now called Halloween, but all its traditions come from the Clan of the Goddess.

But that's not the half of it. There were many minor festivals slotted in between the grander sabbats, and countless celebrations centered around initiations or handfastings. And, of course, there was that venerable institution—the wake—with its host of macabre but riotous "wake games" that young and old alike played, to break the tension and temporarily lift the grief during the three days of the traditional "laying in." It seems any excuse would do for a good time.

Sports were a major part of Celtic tribal life, both for the excitement of competition and for the feel-good fun they bring both to participants and to the boisterous crowd of onlookers. Team competitions, and individual sports to demonstrate strength or skill, were side events at most festivals. They often included combat games, handball, foot races, horse races, and wrestling. Horsemanship often included women competitors in honor of the horse Goddess, Epona. Board games, the most popular of which was called Wooden Wisdom, were similar to today's chess or checkers.

Children walked the fair grounds on high stilts, or played marbles in the dirt. Older children stomped down the tall grasses to make a maze, and the whole tribe played Tread the Maze before sunset ruined their game. In winter, people strapped the bleached shin bone of a horse on the bottom of their boots, and used a long pole to propel themselves around the ice of a pond. In the warm weather, they played a version of tennis, using hands padded and wrapped with leather instead of a racket, to hit the ball back and forth. All games, no matter how trivial or spontaneous, served as an excuse for keen wagering on the part of the bystanders. The lure of gambling remains strong today, and has proven the downfall of many a fine Celt.

Bards, along with their songs, stories, and legends, were a common feature around the nightly campfires. Facility with language was considered an admirable trait, and there were lively contests between the audience and the bards involving punning, feats of memory, and the ability to recite with speed and accuracy. Braziers sizzled with grilled meats, and mead or ale flowed freely.

Throughout the days of the festivities, women gathered to share stories, sing songs, and trade recipes, herbal remedies, and birthing tales, while they openly enjoyed the warmth of female companionship—a time-honored expression of sincere sisterhood—that has never, to this day, lost its heartfelt appeal.

You see, as hard as they worked, as hard as they studied or fought to protect their tribe and keep it safe, the Celts still made plenty of time for merriment. There's a lesson there for all Daughters of the Clan of the Goddess. Set time aside to let go of your cares and worries, to enjoy a much-needed respite. Pencil in some time to kick up your heels and dance to life's fair tune.

The medical advantages of laughter

The ancient healers were on to something when they encouraged all those parties, all those good times, all that frivolity and fun. Laughter is an effective tool for coping with stress. Like the red foam noses cutting through the tension in my university meeting, laughter provides a physical release for accumulated tension and puts a fresh perspective on our troublesome problems.

Even the word "humor" had a double meaning for the ancients, indicating their understanding of its medical significance. They generally considered illnesses to be an interruption in energy flow, or an upset in the bodily fluids which were called "humors." For example, a cheerful person was said to possess a sanguine humor, and a depressed person had a melancholic humor. Even today, we refer to a grouchy person as being in "bad humor," and to lift a person's spirits we are told to "humor them."

Scientifically, studies show the Celtic traditions of fun are good for us. In one extensive study, it was found that laughter lowers the heart rate and blood pressure, and increases a patient's T cell activity, which stimulates the immune system's response to malignant or infected cells. Psychologists have found that laughing at ourselves, or our problems, delivers an empowering sense of detachment and gives us a fresh perspective that diminishes the emotional (and physical) damage stress can cause. Laughter puts us back in control of our lives and situations, and may even release endorphins into our system. It has even been documented that laughter helps prevent or diminish panic attacks. Some healthcare givers are even introducing therapeutic clowns into hospitals. Dr. Patch had it right. So did Dilly. How can you miss? Get more laughter in your stressed-out, frazzled life. As the physical fitness people say, "No more excuses—just do it."

How to find more friends with a sense of humor

Here's an assignment for you. Make a list of all the things, activities, or situations that give you a great deal of pleasure; that gladden your heart and make the world seem a much less serious place. Done? Now make a mental note to put yourself in the way of one of these opportunities for genuine delight at least once a day—you won't regret it.

Assignment 2: Sit down and list all the people you know with a great sense of humor. Some you'll know right off—put a star beside their names and make a pact with yourself to see them more often. Now, the others will be people you've come into contact with at work, or they could be friends of friends you always hear stories about. You may not know them well, or at all. Maybe you've only watched from afar, as others gathered around them regularly burst into spontaneous laughter. It doesn't matter. Consider them all and write down their names, if you know them.

"And what am I supposed to do with this list?" You wonder. Why not incorporate these people into your life? *"C.C. you must be joking! I hardly know some of them."* Well, that's the problem isn't it? If you were a tribal Celt you'd run into them every week or so at the bonfires. You'd dance around the fires, howling with laughter at their latest silly story, wry observation, or ironic insight. Or they'd stitch you up with pratfalls, silly walks, and facial contortions (do you suppose the Celts invented slapstick?). Anyway, they'd be pretty hard to miss unless it was a really huge bonfire. That was then. This is now.

Today, you probably won't just bump into them at a raucous Celtic party, you have to go out and gather them up—like your bouquet of blissful memories. You need a fresh display of light-hearted, fun people who are easy with a smile and a laugh, who aren't afraid to poke fun at serious situations, or laugh at themselves. You know—good folk—not the Nasties who make vicious sport out of laughing at others. Once you find them, embrace them, scoot right over, and make room for them at your feast table. Simple as that and don't balk. Don't be shy. You are a confident Goddess now, a woman in charge of her destiny and, frankly, you are entitled to all the fun there is to be had. You just need to reach out and grab it.

Granted, some of these natural comedians and joy-makers may not be your type at all; maybe you won't share anything in common—that happens. And sometimes (comedians are the first to tell you this) their comic mask may hide a dark and tragic secret. Hmm, that could be problematic. But with others, you will find that it is easy and light to be in their company, and that's the point. You need to muscle your way into their life and claim them as part of your circle of friends. So how do you do that? And where, oh where, do you start?

First, we'll do a bidding spell to draw whimsical, fun-loving energy to you. After that, you be the great huntress. Go out and strike up a conversation. Invite them to lunch or dinner, or throw a party—launch them in amongst your other good friends and cross your fingers. Life's an experiment.

Make it a mission to bring more joy into your life. Call it: Project Lighten Up.

Preparations for the Spell to Draw Laughter

This is your first single-focus spell and it is far less complicated than the other rituals and ceremonies. It's fun, but most effective. You'll need a candle and a mirror to set the candlestick on; herbs to dispel darkness and melancholia; an appropriate incense; and a stone suited to assist in the bidding. That's all. Your tinder box is tiny.

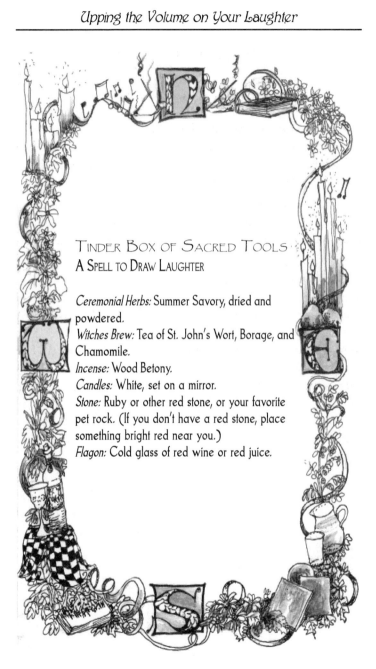

Tinder Box of Sacred Tools
A Spell to Draw Laughter

Ceremonial Herbs: Summer Savory, dried and powdered.

Witches Brew: Tea of St. John's Wort, Borage, and Chamomile.

Incense: Wood Betony.

Candles: White, set on a mirror.

Stone: Ruby or other red stone, or your favorite pet rock. (If you don't have a red stone, place something bright red near you.)

Flagon: Cold glass of red wine or red juice.

A spell to attract more laughter and good times

Unlike your preparation for the full-blown rituals, just bring along the bold confidence of your Personal Power, and a goodly measure of strong intent. In this bidding spell, you will be asking the Goddess to bring more fun and frivolity to your life which, in turn, will lead to greater happiness.

Take an herbal bath if you'd like, though it isn't necessary. Prepare your spell-making site. Set the single white candle in a candlestick on a mirror; place it on a table that will allow you easy eye-contact with the flame.

But wait! Before you do that, I have a rather odd suggestion. You may think I've gone off the deep-end, but it's an old trick the Clan Mothers used to attract something or someone to them. Are you ready? Take the candle and place it in your bare armpit for a moment until it warms slightly. *"For heaven's sake, why?"* I know it's a strange request—weird even—but trust me. Your own scent will help draw special energy to you. It'll be energy that zeroes right in on you; energy that throbs with your own pulse. The happy parties and fun times it draws will always feel comfortable, and the new friends it attracts will feel as if they've known you forever. So indulge me, please.

Okay, now you can set up the candle and light it. Burn some incense, Wood Betony if you can find it, but any will do. Prepare your tea and sip it while you listen to some soothing music and finish setting up. The herbs in the tea will calm you and encourage gladness of heart, while giving depression the royal boot. Place your Ruby or other red stone (or your favorite rock) near the mirror, along with any other red object of your choice. Red draws joy and happiness to you, so if you have a red garment, wear that as well. Now everything is ready.

Turn down the music so you can concentrate. Stand in front of the candle and take three deep breaths, holding for the count of three and exhaling until the air flows clear. Make your Power Fist, say, "Mother-Mine," and squeeze your thumb hard as you feel the Goddess energy shoot up your arm and fill your whole body. Cast your Spell of Protection and see its misty light surround you.

Hold your fist up before you and welcome the Goddess to your spell-bidding. Say, "Mother-Mine, I ask you to attend me, to pull bright energy into my life, that I may live by your sacred principle of enjoying my time on Abred as fully and completely as I am able. Help me this day to welcome the flow of joy, and to open my heart to laughter. Blessed be."

Now make a circle of yellow light with your arms in front of you, clasping your hands as though you are holding a round bushel basket before you. Say, "My body is my sacred circle, laughter and light come gently to me. Move kindly into my circle. Know you are lovingly welcomed into my life. Draw sweetly here to me." Toss the Savory in the air.

Pick up the red stone, or small red object, and repeat the following spell. Say it in a deep, commanding tone, as though it's an official announcement that will be readily accepted as the new rule—the law of the land. When you say the "Spin me" line, spin around once, twice, then thrice as it says. Smile as you spin. Have fun!

Mother-Mine, Knowing One
Draw nigh to me
Spin me happy, spin me fun

Dance me so rightly
Hug me so tightly
Twirl me most happy

Spin me nice
Belly laughs of mine
Rolling laughter so fine
Twirl me most happy
Spin me twice

Happy tears do flow
Vanquished fears all go
Twirl me most happy
Spin me thrice

Friends abound
Joyful sound
Blessed by Three
Blessed be.

Bid adieu to the Goddess. Say, "Great Mother-Mine, grant me a bountiful world brimming with friendship and laughter, song and dance, love and light. Blessed be. And good night."

Let the candle burn for a while in its safe place. Turn up the music again. Get your drink and toast the new life coming to you. When you are ready to blow out the candle, thank it first for lending its magick to your spell. And, finally, place the red object or stone beside your bed that night.

To give the spell a boost, take action as we discussed to draw those fun-filled souls into your circle of friends. And try this: get recommendations from friends on movies they've seen that made them laugh out loud, write down the titles and rent them from your video store. Do the same with books; ask people about the books that made them laugh, then track them down and read them. And by all means, do something spontaneous, like getting people together to hit a comedy club near you. Go after Project Lighten Up with Goddess Gusto, and watch as waves of joy settle into your life like a warm, soft shawl, wrapped snugly around your shoulders. Enjoy, my friend.

Spin a Web of Love

Chapter Nine

Casting Your Net for a Lover...or Two

Aphrodisiacs. Love spells. Love potions. Charms. They were the main reason Celtic women sought guidance and assistance from the herbalists; while the age-old desire to find or to keep a lover kept the early diviners hopping. Things haven't changed much. Today, the telephone and Internet psychics are bombarded with "love problems." It's a fact of life that women, even strong women, accomplished women, spiritual and enlightened women, still love to love.

So, belly up to the Great Love Bar. State your order. Love and drawing love, fixing love, and deepening love—they're all part of the fun on Abred. So, tell me, what can I get you? Is it true love you want? Or is your life so complicated right now that an exciting, no-strings sexual partner would fit the bill? You can be honest. It's your free will to chose whom (and how many loves) you want in your life at any given time. The trick is, of course, to determine exactly what you wish to draw to you—be highly detailed and specific in your list—then rely on the Goddess to crook Her little finger and bring you what you're longing for.

Ancient Celtic traditions of women's sexual freedoms

Women of the Clan of the Goddess lived by very different morals and rules of conduct. Their beliefs were quite the opposite of today's take on sexual roles, and the many rules and restrictions that presently exist were just begging to be broken. Back then, they were much more enlightened and honest about a woman's desires. Added to that, sex had an extra gloss of respectability because it was considered a spiritual act, not simply a physical one. Getting together with a beautiful man was comparable to going to a church or temple. Don't laugh. The act of sexual union was considered sacred—a form of devotion to the Great Mother—for a number of reasons.

First, it echoed Her revered annual mating with the Stag God (or Horned God, or Sun God as he was called in different eras). The divine mating led to the regeneration and rebirth of the entire world, each and every springtime, as evidenced by the budding and growth of plants; the new births among birds and animals, both wild and domestic; and the welcome return of warm weather and longer days. Secondly, the basic Celtic principle of enjoying all the natural pleasures on the earthplane meant that the delights of sex were openly relished, and high on everyone's list of groovy things to do.

Here's another bonus. There was no guilt attached to consensual sex. Their pagan society believed that a healthy and varied sex life, with a number of different partners as you so chose, was a good thing. And this proved practical to the Great Long View. Since many of the tribes were relatively small, any children conceived at multi-tribe festivals or gatherings served to give the limited gene pool a healthy and robust stir.

Of course, with all this sexual activity, it was crucially important for young women to be well-schooled in the reproductive management of their bodies. The herbalists offered a full range of potions, amulets, and superstitions concerning the art of conception; as well as herbal birth control potions and washes, and effective abortifacients should a pregnancy prove dangerous or ill-timed. They even had a trick to temporarily restore virginity—the Celts believed it was renewable in heart and body for new relationships—that involved soaking in a warm shallow bath containing various herbs, often including Lavender and Comfrey. Its effectiveness is still a matter of some speculation.

In the early days, a Celtic woman reared her children with the help of her brother (or brothers), because he knew for certain that each of her children was a blood niece and nephew, no matter who the various fathers were. Among the Clans, not one child was ever cast out, or considered to be inferior, by its legitimacy. But even after the tribes had adopted the custom of lifelong or long time handfastings, everyone was freed of all vows of fidelity during the Goddess's fertility festival—the Beltaine Fires—which marked the long-awaited end of winter. For thousands of years, on that particular festival night, women enjoyed multiple partners of their choice. Throughout the raucous evening, they danced around the bonfires, sometimes in various states of undress, drinking Mead or hallucinogenic drinks from goatskins to intensify and prolong their pleasurable experiences.

But what of the children conceived at this wild, uninhibited spring rite? Not only was no stigma associated with a Beltaine pregnancy, the exact opposite was true—they were venerated. Each was regarded as having been touched by the sacred, and was referred to as a "Child of the Goddess Only."

The identity of the father was of no consequence, since these children were considered to belong to the entire clan. Even the young men conceived during the Beltaine carried this distinction with great pride. When they became warriors, they wore this special "Child of the Mother Only" designation painted proudly on their shields as they went into battle, considering themselves doubly protected against misfortune and harm. Beltaine was also the traditional night to declare divorces, which heightened the sense of liberation and sexual freedom for those particular women who declared that evening.

So those strange springtime stirrings that crooners sing about, those longings that pick up the pace of your heart and heat up the blood, may be vestiges of the old May 1st festival your body can't deny. The restless longings, the sideways glances at handsome men—that desire to kick up your heels—aren't your fault. Oh, no. Blame it on centuries-upon-centuries of wanton Beltaine nights, when the ancestors danced naked around crackling logs that sent sparks roaring up into the night skies above—sparks that touch us still. Yes, blame those irrepressible women, who ventured out with absolute and delightful abandon—it's their fault, not yours. Blame it on your DNA, your natural genetic heritage.

So there. I set you free from the burdens of guilt. Do not apologize for your active and sometimes voracious sexual hungers. Oh no, you are a beautiful sexual being, a direct descendent of all those Clan of the Goddess women who came and danced and slayed the hopelessly romantic hearts of gorgeous men, tens of thousands of years before you. It's their fault. Thank the starry heavens above for that wee miracle.

Decide what kind of sexual relationship suits you best

Yes, you have the right to choose. So allow me to make a grand assumption, just as I did in the last chapter—you want a change. Let's declare out loud, front and center, that your love life could benefit from a small infusion—better yet, a crackling electrical jolt—of fresh energy. Is that fair? (And if you're smugly satisfied with the *status quo*, you'll not be reading any further, will you?)

Let's focus on your sex life. What's your ideal? What do you truly desire? Think about it, before you give me the stock line. Think about your truly private, hush-hush self—what would make her happy? Forget love's stereotypes—the standard brands—think of sexual enjoyment as part of your woman's spirituality. Free yourself from the wet blanket of society's constraints. That's right, change the channel and fine tune the image.

Your sexual and romantic involvements should be as numinous—as sacred—as those moments of enlightenment spent visiting your Nemeton; as joyous as walking with your Spirit Guide; and as empowering as when you acknowledged the presence of your divine self, your Goddess within. That's shocking, isn't it? Sex and spirituality in the same long breath. The newer world religions—those Johnny-come-latelies—thrive on denying, shaming, suppressing, and even hiding all the positive aspects of your natural sexual self. Now I ask you to think of lovemaking as an act of divinity. Wow! That really spins you around doesn't it? Casts it all in a different light—a better light.

And forget guilt. The physical pleasure of a sexual act should not carry a hint of guilt. It should be seen as it is: a pure, natural, healthy, exciting, and highly satisfying tribute to the luminosity of your inner woman self. A tribute to all that is of this earth; all that is of nature. All that is from the Great Mother's loving heart. Convinced? I certainly hope so. Anyway, take my comments seriously, consider them at length, have a good night's sleep, and see if the shoe still fits next morning, Cinderella.

In the meantime, let's talk sex and possible sexual arrangements. Here's one of my experiences. There was a time when I was a single mother with three little children. A professional person with the sole responsibility for raising them, I had little time for dating and absolutely no room in my heart or mind for a serious romantic lover. A good friend, an older gentleman and doctor with whom I worked, suggested I consider bypassing the complexities of younger men who hounded me for romantic commitments, and consider taking on an old lover with no strings attached. (I liked the idea of "taking" a lover, as opposed to the less-active verb of "having" one.)

His suggestion left me in shock. Granted, I'd been plagued by a series of young "lovesick dogs" that proved tiresome and wearing on my emotions. I wasn't seriously interested in any of them, and my dear children, career, house, and long-suffering dog occupied all my waking hours. Yet these young swains, pumped up with hormones and ego, demanded a full romantic involvement. They didn't give up easily, sending flowers and love letters, calling work and threatening to throw themselves under the midnight freight train, and on and on. (My, it makes me sound like a real siren; but I'm sure it has happened to you as well.)

My friend patiently explained that I should change my come-what-may attitude, and start to manage my erotic needs in the same efficient way I handled my job, and raised a little family on my own. Such a liaison, he pointed out, would not compromise my hard-won independence. Rather, I would have much to gain from making uncomplicated, uncommitted love on a regular basis. Then, my handsome older doctor friend stressed that he was not putting himself forward as a possible candidate because, he said with a mischievous smile, his own sex life was already "far too complicated."

I didn't take to the idea. I was still hopelessly romance-driven, convinced that love strikes at random, like lightning—and I suffered for it. At the time, I also couldn't get past the idea that society would frown on such a realistic, almost calculating, approach to sexual relations. But looking back with 20-20 vision, I'd have to say it was excellent advice, foolishly ignored. Imagine how different so many women's lives would be, perhaps even your own, if we approached our body and soul's needs with even a small measure of careful analysis and planning. If we acted to achieve what we really needed. What difference would the proposed older lover have made to my life? Plenty. And who would have known about our arrangement? Absolutely no one. Who was the fool? Not hard. Me.

With this in mind, where are you right now with your sex life? If any possible accommodation or arrangement could be made, what would you like it to be? Consider all the possibilities. Would you sprinkle fairy-dust over your current partner, cast a glamour spell so he wants you like a 22 year old? Or would a secret lover, tucked away in your castle's high round turret, be the solution? You could visit him when you wanted—any time you were ready to shake off life's onerous responsibilities and slip into a filmy negligee. Sound appealing? Or would having not one, but two, completely different lovers suit your tastes? Two lovers, unknown to one another and reflective of separate aspects of your complex soul. It doesn't matter. It's not for me or others to judge.

Just keep in mind that you can design all aspects of your romantic and sexual life the same way you do your life journey.

You are the master designer, the script writer and director for as long as you want to live that kind of life. When it no longer suits you, change it, enhance it, or let it go and choose someone else. Promiscuous? Not to the Clan Mothers' way of thinking. If it is right for your needs and harms no one else—it's a good thing. Period. Keep your cards close to your chest and enjoy.

I have a friend who has chosen to remain single. Unlike the mature lover scenario, it suited her to take on a 19 year old lover who came tapping at her back door, shrouded in the shadows of the porch. At prearranged times, they enjoyed each other to the maximum and then went their separate ways. He had the acquired experience of an older and bolder woman, and she had youthful energy and unbounded sexuality to enjoy at her pleasure. But my doctor friend was right. After a year he declared his undying love—the hormone and ego stew—and, sadly for both, the arrangement came to an end.

So before we cast any spells, and have loads of fun with old love potions and herbal sexual enhancers, decide what it is you'd like to draw to you. What arrangement, or what type of individual, would be ideal for you at this juncture in life's journey? I caution that casting spells to bring a specific person into your arms is fraught with peril, since they may not be right for you. For whatever reason, it may not be a good thing for them (and therefore the two of you), or it may bring heartache and harm to another. Consider this warning and think of a more generic description of an ideal lover, so the universe can select the very best one to meet your requirements. And if religious training or conservative values are important to you, incorporate them into your overall plan. The important point is that you are comfortable with your direction, secure in your decisions, and always in absolute control of your destiny. It's entirely up to you, and the exercise of your own free will.

Believe in your magickal physical attraction

Here is a truism: many people are not beautiful, but something about them—their personality, their way of moving or laughing—makes them extremely attractive. The French actor, Gerard Depardieu, is a case in point. When you simply look at his large nose, his straight hair, and his hang-dog features, you do not consider him attractive. But watch him in action, listen to him speak, read the expression in those eyes, and he becomes as attractive as a god. Wow. In the movie, *Green Card*, Andie Macdowell simply can't resist him, penniless and jobless as he is. But why? Confidence? Yes, for sure. Charm, delivered with twinkling humor? Yes again. An inner light? Absolutely. Once past first impressions, the man is truly beautiful. You want to be in his company.

Now consider this. No matter what you look like, you're not satisfied, right? That is part of the fallout of this society we live in. But Gerard Depardieu didn't let his looks stop him from becoming an international star—even a heartthrob. Nor should anything on your long list of personal physical deficiencies slow you down for a nanosecond. Your attractiveness cannot be altered by changing your eyebrows, or artificially plumping up your lower lip or sagging breasts. Sorry. Save your money for some knock-out clothes, or a trip somewhere exotic, or a course at the college to improve your mind or develop your creative confidence.

Here's a little-known fact. You have incredible animal magnetism that speaks to men. You have wild animal scents that radiate from you in waves, invisible to the naked eye, signals that science has yet to monitor and calibrate, but we know exist. As a woman, you will have been fiercely and hopelessly attracted to a not-so-handsome man—a homely, but irresistibly sexy man—some time in your life. True? Well, suffice to say, you know first-hand such invisible animal magnetism exists.

So where is the source of this indefinable, erotic attraction some people have? It comes from deep, deep inside. It comes from the soul part. And it is delivered with surety and confidence. It is sometimes called "power." You've heard Henry Kissinger's worn out comment that "Power is an aphrodisiac." Well it happens to be true. What you didn't know is this: there are two kinds of power sources for humans—externally created or bestowed power, and internally created power. And that's the best news you'll hear today.

Attaining worldly recognition, or being famous for some serious or frivolous reason, guarantees that you will be seen as outstanding, powerful and, therefore, sexually attractive, and "in demand" (sometimes to hoards of screamers from the opposite sex). That appeal is an externally applied power that works very well, especially in painting you attractive.

But wait, dear friend. The Clan Mothers knew this simple axiom: "Power makes you beautiful." Simple and true. In realizing and unleashing your personal power—your magick soul-developed power—you have begun to project the same attributes and appeal as those who have had power bestowed on them from outside. The confidence you are developing in your internal powers is transmitting invisible waves, transforming you into a numinous spiritual being and suffusing your aura with light. This confidence and inner light cannot help but be reflected on the physical plane.

Now you have two truths to accept: 1) you are divine; and 2) you are indisputably marvelous and sexually attractive to others. So take the hand of your Cosmic Sister who loves a good time, and let's go have some romantic and erotic fun with those two immutable white truths of yours.

Ancient love games and rituals: Most best forgotten

For the fun of it, I've blown the dust off a few ancient tomes so you can see how crazy and desperate some people got when it came to securing a love interest.

Catch a Sparrow. Kill him and eat the brain with your love interest on your mind. Lust will rise within you.

Considering that many birds were considered sacred, the gruesome advice above must have been in response to a most serious and urgent personal need.

Hunt down a wolf. Scrape the marrow from the bone in his left foot and put it inside an amulet to wear near your heart. Then she is sure to love you.

Particularly if she has no olfactory sense. Advice for only the most desperate wolf hunter.

Now for the very worst love charm I ever heard tell of. It comes from ancient writings found in Ireland. I sometimes wonder if it isn't really a bit of off-the-wall Irish humor, meant to startle and entertain, but some people accept it as fact.

The Dead Strip: Sneak into a graveyard at night and exhume a corpse, nine days buried. Tear off a strip of the skin from head to foot. Then crawl into the bedroom of the one ye lust after and, while he is sleeping, wrap this skin around his leg or arm. Take special care to remove it before he wakes up. As long as you secretly keep this skin in your possession, he will only have eyes for you and his lust will be most satisfying.

And now for something completely different. Here's a divination to find out the initial of your true love's name. It was a favorite of mine, handed down from my mother who learned it from her mother. It's a fun kitchen game that passes the time and relieves the drudgery:

Peel an apple with a sharp knife in a circular motion doesil (clockwise) from the top to the bottom, keeping the peel in one single piece without any breaks. (This isn't an easy task for a young girl and my mother got most of her pie apples peeled before I mastered the skill.) Once a long continuous peel is removed from the apple, the young girl says:

> Let me see his letter
> But not his name
> Let him come to me
> With money and fame

Close your eyes and throw the apple peel over your left (spiritual) shoulder. Let another look and tell you what letter it formed. That is the letter of the first name of your true love.

More acceptable love potions, aphrodisiacs and enchantments

What fun potions and aphrodisiacs can be if you don't take them too seriously. As you know, there are many kinds of love as we discussed under the section dealing with what you really desire in a love relationship. Accordingly, the Celts had love potions and aphrodisiacs, as well as amulets, rituals, spells, and charms to suit every occasion. But I think their efficacy had a great deal to do with the motivation and attitude of the user, just as love spells prove most effective when the spellmaker concentrates with laser-beam precision.

Today, we have the option to add a number of modern day accouterments such as essential oils, sensual massage, genital stimulants, and soft, beguiling music for the ultimate experience. As with all love enhancements, it is up to you and your partner to choose, but whatever you agree to use to heighten your pleasure, enjoy without guilt. Consider the experience a divine one.

Here are some herbal love enhancers that were used in the past. You might consider some, but some of the truly archaic ones are best left in time's wastebasket.

Love foods: Love potions

The Celts put great store in herbal or hallucinogenic drinks and special sacred foods, both to arouse desire and to heighten the sexual experience. Lemon, in particular, played a big role in attracting a love partner and we will be using it later in the Spell to Attract a Lover.

To draw down the sensual powers of the universe, an apple was cut through from stem to bottom, revealing the seeds inside and a design reminiscent of a woman's genitals. As a prelude to lovemaking, a couple would take bites from the apple, then rub its moist and fragrance flesh all over each other's bare bodies. Or pieces might be bitten from the apple and hidden in various places on one partner or both, then nibbled on as they were discovered. Hidden where? In places restricted only by the lovers' imaginations. Wow, forget about pies, sauce, and cider vinegar.

Hazel nuts were also considered lust elevators. In a solemn ritual, each partner would eat nine Hazel nuts, the last three being plucked from one another's mouth. The nuts were believed to have strong arousal properties to awaken love in each participant.

Periwinkle flowers and leaves held a special place in love rituals. It was believed that a couple who ate them together would enjoy a lasting love, one that would grow and flourish. Add some to your salad tonight, but be careful—if it works as well as they believed, you'd better be absolutely sure your dinner partner is your one and only love.

Fruit, nuts, and flowers. Wild claims. Wilder results. Whoever would have thought?

Potions were a closely-guarded secret of the love spellmaker, and an effective one could increase the line-up of clients at her cottage door. Some potions were used as part of a beckoning spell, some were used to bind a romantic love to the spellmaker, and others to provoke lust in either or both of the partners. There was an arsenal of herbs that were believed to draw romance when drunk in a potion. They included: Herb William, Chamomile, crushed Cumin seeds, and Lemon, as juice or as the herb Lemon Balm. All had specially focused energy, and the addition of the Chamomile brought assurance of success. Brew some up, what do you have to lose?

Aphrodisiacs, hidden fragrances, oils, and enchantments

For the randy ones amongst us with thoughts of lust rather than long term romance, or for those whose lifelong love could use an energetic boost in the bedroom, the following herbs were known to arouse amorous feelings.

As an aphrodisiac, the early Celtic herbalist would whip up a concoction that was sure to include: Summer Savory leaves; Rocket seeds (also known as the salad plant, Arugula); carrot seeds bruised and steeped in hot water; and the sacred herb Vervain, that had first been boiled in white wine. Mix them all together in a drink, and adjust or add natural flavorings to taste. Drink it half an hour before the lovemaking is set to begin.

Enhancements like body massage oils were recommended to heighten sensation. They used a Rose base, often a Cabbage Rose Oil, that was said to aid those who lacked enthusiasm in the act of lovemaking. Today, massage specialists still favor a Rose oil in an almond oil carrier for sensual massage that leads to sweet lovemaking.

Hidden fragrances and genital stimulants were also part of the early tribal woman's repertoire. The pure oil of the Marshmallow flower was a popular one for rubbing on genitals to increase physical sensation. It was also common for a woman to slather a mixture of honey and blackberries between her "love lips" to surprise and delight her lover and to promote arousal in both. This was an earlier version of the perfumed or flavored sprays and oils available for this purpose today. Modern "love shops" stock a whole range of such supplies, including the imported Kava Kava that is said to be an effective stimulator of sexual response when taken as a drink and/or massaged onto the sex organs of either or both partners.

Preparations for the Attraction Spell that will cast your net

Enough of strange aphrodisiacs, gruesome charms, and assorted lust-builders from the past. It's time to get serious about attracting the romance, love, and—yes—satisfying sex you have determined is right for you at this moment in your life. The beckoning spell that follows will open up the energy lines to draw your heart's desire. This spell has a particular magnetic energy and requires intense concentration. To ensure that your intent is pure and true, it is best not to name names—the universe may have someone even better suited to you in mind! Also, unlike other spells, it's more effective to put a time limit on the spell. Let's say a time span measured by nature—one full cycle of the moon, or until the turning of the leaves or the first skiffs of winter snow. Now, it is essential that you prepare yourself and pledge to do the following three things:

1. Believe strongly in the positive outcome, and know the Goddess blesses your act of drawing love into your life.

2. Concentrate on your ideal loved one (or two) over a few days prior to the spell. Vividly image them and the many aspects of their love for you.

3. Expect love to arrive. That's all. Don't moon over it, second guess it or worry about it. Expect it. Period.

Quick Minute Magick: Casting your love net

Those of you who are the Quick-meisters know the general format: Squeeze your Power Fist, cast your Spell of Protection, and imagine all that you read to be true. And it will be. It has worked before and it will again. Enjoy the love and fun coming to your private life.

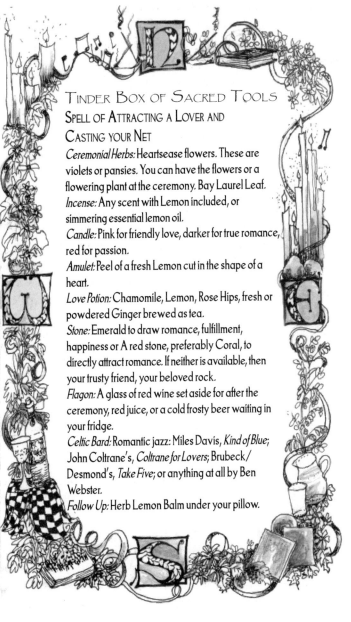

Tinder Box of Sacred Tools

Spell of Attracting a Lover and Casting your Net

Ceremonial Herbs: Heartsease flowers. These are violets or pansies. You can have the flowers or a flowering plant at the ceremony. Bay Laurel Leaf.

Incense: Any scent with Lemon included, or simmering essential lemon oil.

Candle: Pink for friendly love, darker for true romance, red for passion.

Amulet: Peel of a fresh Lemon cut in the shape of a heart.

Love Potion: Chamomile, Lemon, Rose Hips, fresh or powdered Ginger brewed as tea.

Stone: Emerald to draw romance, fulfillment, happiness or A red stone, preferably Coral, to directly attract romance. If neither is available, then your trusty friend, your beloved rock.

Flagon: A glass of red wine set aside for after the ceremony, red juice, or a cold frosty beer waiting in your fridge.

Celtic Bard: Romantic jazz: Miles Davis, *Kind of Blue*; John Coltrane's, *Coltrane for Lovers*; Brubeck/Desmond's, *Take Five*; or anything at all by Ben Webster.

Follow Up: Herb Lemon Balm under your pillow.

Significance of the Sacred Tools

Heartsease, which is a sweet violet sometimes called wild pansy, is especially significant. The Celts believed nothing surpassed it for love spells, and for drawing the very best to your own heart. The plant was also commonly known among them as, "Call Me to You and Cuddle Me." You can pick up a small plant at your florist or pluck the flowers from your garden. It should be present at your ritual, or at least represented by a picture or a painting. Bay Laurel leaves also draw love when that is your intent. Place a dried leaf from your kitchen cupboard in front of the burning candle.

The candle may be white for the sacred, that's always a safe choice. But Patricia Telesco in *Exploring Candle Magick* recommends you chose a shade on the red spectrum that represents the exact type of love you wish to draw. She suggests soft pink for a warm, friendly love, and the various shades in between all the way to deep, intense red for passionate love. She also suggests you carve a heart in the candle itself. If you have Lemon essential oil, anoint the candle with it to further enhance the magick. As with the last spell, set the candle on a mirror. Watch the flame in the mirror and touch its reflection there. Fire was once considered the ultimate magick, and you now draw on that magick without being burned. You too are magickal.

As you can see, Lemon is the key ingredient in this beckoning spell. Its pungent oil, distinct fragrance and magical properties radiate into the universe and bid your lover attend you. Either use an incense that has Lemon in it, or make your own (see the Appendix). If you have the essential oil, daub it on your wrists and your temples. The tea, or Love Potion, has lemon flavoring. Use freshly squeezed lemon juice or a lemon flavored herbal tea bag if you wish, along with the herb Chamomile for success; Rose hips for the tried-and-true love benefits of the Rose; and Ginger for special success relating to love wishes. Your amulet, to be with you during the spell and also placed before your candle, is carved from the fresh peel of a Lemon. Even your follow up includes placing Lemon Balm under your pillow. The Clan Mothers believed strongly in the abilities of Lemon Balm to capture an appropriately lusty lover, and to bring him to share that very pillow with you. Nice thought. Happy times ahead.

The stones should be an Emerald or a piece of Red Coral, if possible. If not, we can enhance the energy in the beckoning spell by having your already personally energized favorite rock beside you.

The Bard can be one of any of the CDs I mention. Jazz is known to penetrate the various layers of consciousness and alter your reality, so I recommend soft jazz if you can find it. It has been said that more people have made love listening to Paul Desmond's saxophone on *Take Five* than to any other record in print. *Kind of Blue* by Miles Davis is probably a close second. Try to find one of these or use your favorite romantic music.

Before you start the beckoning spell ceremony, read the spell, and feel free to adjust it by adding a verse, or writing your own. And don't forget that you, my friend, are a strong energy force. You are capable of moving the clouds, parting the rolling fog, and drawing the best partner to you. And be clear in your mind that it is a partner who is suited to you, and free to be with you.

Begin your woman's spell to draw a love into your life

Start the music. Make up your love potion and bring it to the living room. Set up your candle and light it. Blow softly on the flame to remind yourself that the Goddess fills your lungs with the element of sweet air. Touch the flame's reflection in the mirror and consider what is real and what is not. Place the Bay Laurel Leaf in front of the candle. Kiss it for good fortune. Start the incense and put the magick stone close beside your chair. Place the heart-shaped Lemon peel amulet in your hand. Relax while you listen to the music and sip your love potion. Breathe in the steam water and imagine the blend of herbs adding to your animal magnetism, to your drawing energy. Love is out there. You are going to draw exactly the kind of love you desire. (Not "want." Never say "want.") Put the spell close beside you. Read it over while you sip the potion. Get the cadence, its chant-like lyricism. Adjust one of the option verses to suit your situation, or compose your own. You can't go wrong when your intentions are sterling and your heart is pure.

When you are relaxed and feel ready, place the Lemon heart amulet over your heart, pat it three times and then place it with the Bay leaf in front of your candle. Turn the music down.

Stand before the flaming candle. Take three deep breaths, holding each for the count of three and exhaling. Imagine the air growing clearer each time you exhale. You are cleansed. The Goddess breathes you divinely pure. Cast your Spell of Protection, seeing your body surrounded by shimmering misty light. Be sure it is in place and you are comfortable and serene. Make the Power Fist with your left hand and squeeze hard. Feel the Goddess energy surge up your arm and flood your body.

Hold your Power Fist straight up in front of you and greet the Goddess, "Welcome, Mother-Mine. I ask you to fill me up with magnetic energy, that I may draw love into my life. Love that benefits me, and pleases me, and fills me up with all that is good and pleasurable. Help me this day to draw sweet love into my heart. Blessed be."

Take your left open palm and press it to your forehead. Say, "New love (or renewed love) fill my mind with thoughts of delight." Press your open palm to your heart. Say, "Lover mine, touch my heart with your tenderness." Then cup both your breasts with your hands and say, "Lover caress my breasts and lay your sweet, loving head peacefully on my chest."

Then place one hand over the other in the area of your genitals, and say, "Lover, beautiful lover, fill me up with passion and pleasure." Open both arms as though your have someone in front of you, and say, "Come to me with all that is good and fitting, bring me bushels of carnal pleasures, bring me deep and heartfelt joy, bring your love to me unencumbered."

As with the last spell, you are making a declaration to the universe. It will hear your forceful delivery and do as you command. Pick up and hold your stone, and read or say the following spell substituting whatever you feel is appropriate, where appropriate:

> **Lover of mine**
> **Hear my call**
> **My lovely One**
> **With soft footfall**
> **Come run to me.**
>
> **Heat of my flesh**
> **Flames rush high**
> **My naked One**
> **Draw thee nigh**
> **Come lie with me**
>
> **By my Mother's tide**
> **By her full moon face**
> **My precious One**
> **Let love take place**
> **Come here to me**
>
> **Hand in Hand**
> **Breast to breast**
> **Heart beat heart**
> **Goddess blessed**
> **Come love me**
>
> **Blessed be**

If it is definitely a lifelong love you seek to draw to you, and a happy and long lasting union that you most desire, add this last stanza:

> By the coupling of geese
> Forever as one
> By the silver light of Moon
> Joined together, forever, anon
> Blessed fair by thee
> Blessed be
> Lover, Stay by me.

Bid farewell to the Goddess. Say, "Mother-Mine, grant me this love that I so desire. To fill me up and to calm my soul, that I may move through Abred with a light and dancing step. Blessed be. And Good night."

Lean over and blow out the candle, letting the smoke from the wick bathe your face. Pick up your glass of wine, or get your cold beer from the fridge, and make a toast to the one who is—right this moment—making his way to you. Be strong and sure of heart, for love is coming.

When you go to bed, put some Lemon Balm under the pillow and imagine that your lover's sweet face will soon be there beside you. You will feel so happy, so very good. Best wishes to both of you—or all of you!

C. C. bids you fond farewell

It has been a fine and pleasurable journey for me, walking beside you and sharing all that has been passed down from the Clan Mothers, the wisewomen and the Druidic sages of ancient times. And it has been a heartfelt thrill to stand by as you accessed deep personal and spiritual strength through practicing the ancient women's mysteries and secrets of the Clan of the Goddess. You will never again think of yourself as a victim for you have touched the fingertips of your Goddess, and most important of all, you've come to truly believe in yourself. You never cease to amaze.

I would like to leave you with an interpretation from *The Secret Rites and Traditions of Ancient Britain Restored* by Lewis Spence, that I find inspiring. It's a translation from archaic Gaelic texts that were originally recorded in the Celtic *Blue Book*. As always, the text is composed of three triads, leading to the sacred number nine. The three sets are called the deliverances, the excellences, and the attainments. They speak of what to expect after your life journey here is completed and the next great adventure in Avalon begins. It is full of ancient good news, and I think it will leave you on a high note to think of heaven in this way. Oh, and don't forget that heaven, called *Gwynvyd* in the ancient language, is only the middle of your excellent adventure. You have much to look forward to, dear friend.

Your three deliverances to expect in Avalon:

> There will be no transgression which will not be set right.
> There will be no displeasures which will not be forgiven.
> There will be no anger which will not be satisfied.

In Avalon, you will be comforted with these three excellences:

> There will be nothing ill-favored which shall not be adorned.
> There will be no evil which shall not be removed.
> There will be no desire which shall not be attained.

And when you reach this peaceful state of being, there are three more glorious attainments awaiting:

> There can be nothing which shall not be known.
> There can be no loss of anything beloved which shall not be regained.
> There can be no end to Gwynvyd.

So be it. The best is yet to come. Blessed be.

And remember when you some day cross over to the lush apple orchard of the Otherworld—our home in Avalon—the Clan Mothers will be there to greet you, to embrace you tenderly, and to welcome you with sisterhood, warmth and caring. It will be as if you've always known and loved these wisewomen. They will remind you that "You are never alone."

But before that happy day, promise yourself that you'll make the very best of your allotted time on the earthplane. Believe in your personal storehouse of magick; open yourself to expand your soul; fill your heart with plenty of love and joy; and for goodness sake, don't forget to kick up your heels and indulge in the many sweet pleasures of Abred.

You are magical, you are divine, you are loved.

Blessed be.

Appendix

The Goddess Goes to the Grocery Store

A list of herbs used in the rituals

Wherever possible, use fresh herbs and plenty of them. If you stock up on dried herbs, rub them in your palms to release their fragrance and magick before using them. Don't be put off by the cost per pound or kilo of these herbs, a small bag weighs little, so your cost won't be prohibitive.

Some of these ingredients can be purchased as essential oils, which is quite convenient for the bathtub. I've listed them as they appear in the book, and I've put a star beside those you may already have in your kitchen spice rack or your herbal tea cupboard:

Borage
Chamomile-tea bags or
    loose *
Sage *
Basil *
Bay Laurel Leaves *

Horehound
Mugwort
Red Clover-tea bags or
    loose *
Lavender
Parsley *

Star Anise
Fennel *
Cinnamon Stick *
Sweet Paprika *
Ginger *
St. John's Wort
Comfrey
Motherwort

Rosemary *
Herb Bennet
Vervain
Valerian
Agrimony
Summer Savory *
Wood Betony
Rose hips
Lemon Balm

Magick stones

Hunt through your jewelry box (and your mother's and your best friends') for some of these semi-precious stones to use in the ceremonies. Others can be found in natural form (or polished and unmounted) in a good rock shop.

Your own favorite Rock
Amber
Amethyst
Opal
Turquoise

Sapphire
Ruby (or other red stone)
Emerald
Coral

Making your own incense

You can whip up a batch of incense in your own kitchen. Use these fragrance sticks or cones in your rituals and ceremonies, or give them away as love gifts. If you have a friend who needs calming, mix up those particular herbal ingredients. A friend who wants to be more visionary in all they do? Check back to the chapter dealing with visionary herbs and mix them all together. You can have a blast and do lots of good for those you love.

Chose the herbs that fit with particular spells, or have properties for healing, or for enhancing love, success and magick in your life. Toss in some other sweet or pleasant-smelling herb like Lavender or Sandalwood essential oil for the fun of it.

When you are satisfied with your combination of herbal ingredients, grind them all together in a coffee mill or blender until they are fine or almost powdered. Add Acacia Gum or Gum Arabic a bit at a time until the mixture firms up and adheres to itself. I find these binding gums at my local art supply store.

You can form your handmade incense into narrow stand-up cones with your fingers and let them dry for 24 hours. For the more commercial-looking stick variety, take a small wooden skewer that you use on the BBQ, or a good stout natural (not plastic) broom straw, and press the mixture around the stick and smooth it out. Let these dry on waxed paper. You'll find you are almost giddy from working so closely with the different powdery herbs, and that's a nice side benefit.

If you wish, you can get fancy and add color or sparkles, just be sure they can handle the smoldering and won't flare up in flames. And whatever you do, don't forget music while you work, and have a glass of wine at the ready to celebrate your creative accomplishment, just as your Clan Mothers taught you.

Bibliography

Chin-Yee, Fiona. *Sam's Story*. Halifax: Project Sam Publishing, 1988.

Couzyn, Jeni. *House of Changes*. Heinemann, 1978.

Estes, Dr. Clarissa Pinkola. *Women Who Run With the Wolves*. New York: Ballantine Books, 1992.

Gawain, Shakti. *Creative Visualization*. New York: Bantam Books, 1982.

Hammerschlag, Carl A. *The Dancing Healers: A Doctor's Journey of healing with Native Americans*. San Francisco: Harper, 1988.

Reade, W. Winwood. *The Veil of Isis or Mysteries of the Druids*. North Hollywood, CA: Newcastle Publishing, 1992.

Roman, Sanaya and Packer, Duane. *Opening to Channel*. Tiburon, CA: H. J. Kramer, 1987.

Skelton, Robin. *The Practice of Witchcraft*. (rev. ed.) Victoria, BC: Press Porcepic, 1990.

Skelton, Robin. *Spellcraft*. Toronto: McClelland and Stewart, 1978.

Spence, Lewis. *The Mysteries of Britain*. North Hollywood, CA: Newcastle Publishing, 1993.

Telesco, Patricia. *Exploring Candle Magick.* New Jersey: New Page, 2001.

Wilde, Lady. *Ancient Cures, Charms and Usages of Ireland.* Detroit: Singing Tree Press, 1970.

Some other favorite books worth mentioning:

Baring, Anne and Cashford, Jules. *The Myth of the Goddess.* New York: Penguin (Arkana), 1993.

Bunney, Sarah ed. *The Illustrated Book of Herbs.* London: Octopus, 1984.

Condren, Mary. *The Serpent and the Goddess: Women, Religion and Power in Celtic Ireland.* San Francisco: Harper & Row, 1989.

Cowan, Tom. *Fire in the Head: Shamanism and the Celtic Spirit.* San Francisco: Harper, 1993.

Ody, Penelope. *The Complete Medicinal Herbal.* Toronto: Key Porter Books, 1993.

Walker, Barbara G. *The Crone: Woman of Age, Wisdom and Power.* New York: Harper & Row, 1985.

Walker, Barbara G. *The Woman's Encyclopedia of Myths and Secrets.* San Francisco: Harper, 1983.

ndex

About the Author and Illustrator

C. C. Brondwin is a professional woman who has been honored as an award-winning documentary journalist in both print and broadcast, and who has served as a senior executive at two universities, one a women's institution. Brondwin was raised as a spiritualist in a Celtic family where ceremony and ritual, talismans and amulets, were a part of her daily life. Both her mother and grandmother were recognized diviners and mystics. These inherited women's gifts of "knowing" led Brondwin on a spiritual quest to discover the Celtic Goddess of her ethnic roots. She studied herbalism and homeopathic medicine and traveled to Britain to rediscover the power and the dynamism of early Clan Mothers who worshipped the Mother Goddess as Briganntia, or Brigit. Her dream is to recreate a far-reaching network of spiritual elders to serve as Clan Mothers to young women today.

She lives in the sunny foothills of the Canadian Rockies with her husband, artist and editor, William Johnson and their Newfoundland dog, Zimba. Visit C. C.'s website at *www.ccbrondwin.com.*

Christine Ahmad is a self-taught artist and an instructor in paper art. Born in England, her whimsical drawings are inspired by her delight at growing up with the daily myths of the little people. Christine lives in the countryside with her husband Mo, and their two adopted dogs, Philby and Sam. Her home and studio are snuggled in a cozy grove of trees with a glorious mountain view just outside C. C.'s hometown.